Twayne's United States Authors Series

Sylvia E. Bowman, *Editor*

INDIANA UNIVERSITY

Ellery Channing

ELLERY CHANNING

By ROBERT N. HUDSPETH

Pennsylvania State University

 **223**

Twayne Publishers, Inc. :: New York

FOR KAY

Preface

Any study of a "minor" figure is menaced from two sides: the critic is tempted first to make more out of a modest literary achievement than the work will bear; then he is, in reaction, tempted to treat the whole subject with disdain and push on to a mechanical conclusion merely to rid himself of the task. In this study of Ellery Channing, I have tried to avoid these two unsatisfactory alternatives by reminding myself that two of the most discriminating minds of the nineteenth century—Henry Thoreau and Ralph Waldo Emerson—admired, respected, and loved him.

In my attempt to understand the poet, I have been guided by five broad aims. First, I desire to recover and assess the story of his life to discover the tensions and ambitions that first shaped and then alternately guided and thwarted him. Second, I try to see his prose as the record of a typical, young, New England writer coming into his intellectual maturity in the late 1830's and early 1840's, as the record of a man defining the possibilities of an intellectual life, and as the record of how Thoreau became a living symbol of a value-laden way of living. Third, I read his poetry closely so that we may see what values motivated Channing—see in perspective the significance of his rejection of urban America and his desire for more subjective standards of living. Fourth, I follow his attempt to apply in his longer poems this standard of value to New England as a region. Fifth, I show the importance of Channing to his friends—Nathaniel Hawthorne, A. Bronson Alcott, Margaret Fuller, Thoreau, and Emerson—to understand how he enriched their lives, to grasp the importance of conversation as a form of intellectual activity, and to show the never-failing interest in "friendship" as a theme among the Concord writers.

To achieve these ends, I have used three approaches: first, I have drawn on the manscript letters of Channing and his friends to write a biographical essay demonstrating the attitudes and psychic traits that made him the man he was. Second, I have examined closely his writing, both prose and poetry, to understand the assumptions behind it and to show the implications of what he wrote. I have not considered it necessary to defend Channing's weaknesses nor to plead for his merit as a writer: his poetry has self-evident limitations, but these should not deter us from understanding the significance of his life and vocation. Nor have I discussed his many unpublished poems—those he published are fully representative of his work. Third, I have focused on the intellectual history of Concord during the 1840's and 1850's by using Channing as a point of reference. Because he was often discussed and remembered by his contemporaries, we have a detailed record of what he added to this community of the imagination. In fact, his friendship became his most lasting contribution to that community.

Channing's position as friend, confidant, and poet puts him squarely in the midst of America's most imaginative literary period. His own talent sometimes failed to meet our standards of literary excellence, but he persists both as a symbol and as a man of unusual personal magnetism. He was one of those men, who, in Arthur Schlesinger's words, "must dream broadly and guilelessly, if only to balance those who never dream at all."

My work has left me indebted to many people for help and encouragement. The staff of the Syracuse University Library was particularly generous and unfailingly helpful, especially Miss Marian Mullins and Mrs. Geneva Lewis. I received the assistance of Miss Carolyn Jakeman, Miss Judy Andrea, and Mrs. Christie Richter of the Houghton Library and of Mrs. Marcia Moss, Mrs. George Barker, Mrs. Marion Hayward, and Mr. Edwin Diffley of the Concord Free Public Library. Mr. Rodney Dennis, III, of the Houghton Library, Mr. Herbert Cahoon of the Morgan Library, Mr. Thomas Casteen of the University of Virginia, and Mrs. Christine Hathaway of Brown University have all helped provide reproductions of Channing's manuscripts.

To Bob and Jeanne Hill I am grateful for hospitality, good humor, and patience in always having room for a tired researcher. My friends and colleagues, David Lyttle, David Owen, Thornton Parsons, Roger B. Stein, and Richard Baldwin have all had the kindness to read the manuscript at various stages and give me their advice (though all the errors and shortcomings remain mine alone). I am particularly indebted to Walter Sutton for his encouragement, patience, and friendship and especially for his example as a scholar and a teacher. To my wife Kay, I dedicate this book with the knowledge that it is but a small token for her part in its creation.

ROBERT N. HUDSPETH

Pennsylvania State University
University Park, Pennsylvania

Acknowledgments

For permission to quote from the letters and manuscripts of William Ellery Channing, I wish to thank John C. Fuller. For permission to quote from the letters and manuscripts of Margaret Fuller, I would like to thank Mr. Fuller and Mr. and Mrs. Willard P. Fuller. I acknowledge with thanks the permission of the following institutions to quote from manuscripts in their possession: the Harvard College Library, the Concord Free Public Library, the Massachusetts Historical Society, the Harris Collection of American Poetry and Plays in the Brown University Library, the Pierpont Morgan Library, the Clifton Waller Barrett Library of the University of Virginia Library, the Huntington Library of San Marino, California. Mr. Richard L. Herrnstadt and Mrs. F. Wolsey Pratt have given me permission to quote from the letters of A. Bronson Alcott. I would like to thank Mr. Kenneth Walter Cameron, editor of *The Emerson Society Quarterly,* for permission to quote from two essays of mine published in that journal.

Contents

Chronology

1817   William Ellery Channing born November 29, in Boston, Massachusetts, second of four children born to Dr. Walter Channing and Barbara Perkins Channing.

1824   Enrolls at Round Hill School.

1834   Enters Harvard. Leaves college before Christmas; retreats to relatives' home on the Artichoke River.

1839   Moves to McHenry County, Illinois, where he begins a homestead farm.

1840   Sells his land and moves to Cincinnati. Begins to publish poems in *The Dial.*

1841   Meets Ellen Fuller to whom he is married, September 24.

1842   The Channings move to Massachusetts. Friendships with Emerson and Thoreau begin.

1843   The Channings settle in Concord. *Poems* published.

1844   Channing works briefly for Horace Greeley's New York *Tribune.* First child, Margaret Fuller Channing born May 23.

1846   Trip to Italy in March. Caroline Sturgis Channing born April 13.

1847   *Conversations in Rome* and *Poems: Second Series* published.

1849   Birth of Walter Channing, April 14. *The Woodman, and Other Poems* published.

1850   Death of Margaret Fuller Ossoli, July 14.

1853   Birth of Giovanni Eugene Channing, June 10. Separation of Ellery and Ellen Channing on November 18. She goes to Worcester, Massachusetts, to live with Thomas W. Higginson and his wife.

1855   Reunion with Ellen. Channing works for New Bedford *Mercury.*

1856   Henry Channing born June 15. Ellen Channing dies, September 22.
1858   *Near Home* published.
1862   Thoreau dies.
1864   Channing and Sophia Thoreau edit Thoreau's *Cape Cod* and *The Maine Woods*.
1871   *The Wanderer* published.
1873   *Thoreau: The Poet-Naturalist* published.
1885   *Eliot, A Poem* published.
1886   *John Brown and the Heroes of Harper's Ferry* published.
1901   William Ellery Channing dies, December 23, in Concord.
1902   *Poems of Sixty-Five Years* published, edited by F. B. Sanborn.

CHAPTER 1

The Making of a Poet

THE day after Christmas, 1901, Thomas Wentworth Higginson interrupted his holiday vacation to attend the funeral of an obscure recluse in nearby Concord. Returning to Boston, he absentmindedly wrote a diary entry for the twenty-fifth: "to Ellery Channing's funeral—a placid close of a sad life."[1] Higginson, Channing's cousin and brother-in-law, had good reason to call his kinsman's life sad: he had come in moments of crisis to rescue Channing's wife and children when the marriage failed; he watched the children grow up with neither father nor mother; he read volume after volume of Channing's poetry when seemingly no one else cared to read them. A sad life indeed!

But the smooth, untroubled mind that made Higginson successful—that brought him all the public accolades that eluded Channing—never understood the esteem which Emerson, Thoreau, Alcott, and Margaret Fuller showered on Channing. At a time when poetry counted for little in a thriving America, Channing stubbornly held to a vision of what man might be, a vision of the possibilities that eluded the captives of a middle-class culture. In the face of formidable personal tensions and frustrations, Channing wrote and published hundreds of lines of poetry; he was Thoreau's first biographer; and, more importantly, he enriched one of America's most unique, productive literary groups—the friends who made "Concord" synonymous with literary distinction.

I *The Inheritance*

When William Ellery Channing was born on November 29, 1817, no one would have given too much thought to his future. His family was so well established in professional and mercantile careers that anything but a continuation of the family traditions would be unthinkable. The father, Dr. Walter Channing, an innovative, brilliant obstetrician was soon to become Professor of Obstetrics and Medical Jurisprudence of the Harvard Medical School. He had married Barbara Perkins, a daughter of the powerful, immensely wealthy merchant clan. Moreover, the Channings were as impressive intellectually as the Perkins were financially. Descended from William Ellery, Rhode Island's signer of the Declaration of Independence, the Channings were represented by such men as William Ellery Channing, New England's most influential minister, and Edward Tyrell Channing, Harvard's Boylston Professor of Rhetoric, a man who impressed the minds of uncounted Harvard graduates, including Emerson and Thoreau.[2]

So in two directions Ellery (as the family called him to distinguish the boy from his uncle) found his family defending, increasing, and directing the Boston culture which was developing from the shadows of the "Second War of Independence." This Boston had slowly turned from the rigors of Congregational orthodoxy to the more benign creeds of Unitarianism and, simultaneously, had come to dominate the marketplace. Salem, once a rival for economic power, was withering; capital investments, long ignored by the Yankee shippers, were thriving. As America entered the industrial revolution amid the din of cotton mills and shoe factories, Boston led the way. What could be brighter for any new citizen: a pinched religion had given way to humane reasoning; an unstable young republic now had found its economic and political strength. Almost overnight, the tyranny of Calvin and of Britain had been eased. But with this freedom was growing a new tyranny of the spirit; the god of compensation was busily at work. Material and spiritual ease had indeed been won, but emotional sterility and material complacency came implacably.

Little Ellery had a delightful home among a growing family. He had leisure to play; he had affection and love to comfort him. But, with an appalling suddenness, his life was shattered when he was only five by the death of his mother, Barbara Channing. Suddenly he found himself shunted to relatives or friends at a time when he most needed security. Even when Dr. Channing married Elizabeth Wainwright, Ellery showed the marks of his mother's death in moodiness and intractable stubbornness.

During these years the boy was deprived of the purposive discipline that might have taught his independent and exuberant spirit how to benefit from its innate energy. Instead, he grew to maturity never knowing that "responsibility" was an honest virtue, that the world rightfully demanded a self-control over impulses of the moment.

Channing learned early to love books: he frequented the Boston Athenaeum; he had the liberty of George Ticknor's immense library, and he earned a family reputation for bookish solitude. His father sent him in 1827 to the Round Hill School newly founded by Joseph G. Cogswell and George Bancroft. After a year of this experimental education, Channing attended various Boston-area academies; and in 1834 he enrolled in Harvard's class of 1838 with only a "condition" in arithmetic.[3]

Channing had every right to a Harvard degree, and he had all the social and intellectual connections to make his entry a routine event. True, his father and Uncle Edward had been involved in one of Harvard's several "rebellions," but they had recovered to take their proper station later in life. These four years for Ellery were to be the preparation for a career of his choice (Dr. Walter was adamant that his son should choose his vocation, that he should not be forced into a life of medicine). But almost no experience could have suited Ellery Channing less than entrance to Harvard. The college was still blighted with the curricular restrictions of President Quincy. The dullest of recitation systems and most pernicious of marking schemes had withstood the assaults of even so powerful an academic as George Ticknor. The college expected of its students, in Van Wyck Brooks's phrase, "a clear, distinct mentality, a strong distaste for nonsense, steady composure, a calm and gentle demeanour."[4] Such a life was made of character traits foreign to Ellery Channing who was bookish but undisciplined, intelligent but willful, honest but emotionally erratic. He barely lasted at Harvard until Thanksgiving. On December 4, 1834, Channing left Harvard and fled to a gristmill on the Artichoke River where, among distant relatives, he found a life more to his taste. Later overtures of reconciliation from the college and from Dr. Channing had no effect; Ellery Channing had ended his formal education.[5]

The short, almost comic, encounter with Harvard was a decisive and symbolic event in Channing's life. At a time when he was irrevocably to assume a family role through a reputable career, Channing chose to withdraw, leave all the traditions and roles which a Harvard degree represented, and find for himself a unique life. To leave Harvard was to reject Boston as well as his family. With strong strokes he, in his first of many acts of rebellion, severed the connection between his family's expectations and his own sense of values: Harvard stood for tradition, Channing wanted fresh experience; Harvard demanded intellectual discipline, Channing prized the inspiration of the moment; Harvard was socially respectable, Channing cared nothing for society. Before he was twenty, he was showing the character traits that enriched and tormented his life throughout the rest of the century.

Having made the act of rebellion, he fell into habitual idleness. He might have rejected the ideals of his family, but he did return to his father's house where, for almost five years, he lived a strangely passive life. Though he read voraciously in the German and English Romantics—Johann G. von Herder, Friedrich Klopstock, Johann Wolfgang Goethe, George Gordon Byron, and William Wordsworth—his intellectual life remained as dormant as his daily routine. Little in his writing shows any deep impact that these writers might have made, for they urged him into a life of poetic activity rather than into a particular intellectual or esthetic point of view. From these years came a heightened, unshakable resolve to write. He traveled desultorily in New Hampshire and New York as he turned over his future in his mind. Only a brief, tentative outburst of writing for the Boston *Mercantile Journal* interrupted the idleness of these years. In the spring and summer of 1835, a series of erratic poems and essays appeared from the pen of "Hal Menge," as Channing called himself.[6] During this time, he found that all the other possibilities of a career faded before the one grand vision of poetry. To be a poet was a goal worthy of the human spirit. He had found a world of values, aspirations, and emotional satisfactions that had wholly vanished from mercantile and Unitarian Boston.

II *The West*

For several months in 1838 and 1839, Channing had talked of going to the frontier of Illinois. A friend, Josiah Dwight, had made a life by homesteading; an uncle, James H. Perkins, had

found the West invigorating. This world, free from the crabbed
points of view of Boston and Cambridge, had the spaces and the
opportunities to make a poet dream. Finally, in the fall of 1839,
Channing made the long, arduous trip from Boston to Illinois by
coach, barge, and steamboat, arriving at Dwight's farm in
McHenry County. The land, he found, was desolate, the terrain
grim. "When I first saw Chicago," he recalled, "there were no
houses on the other side of the river, and there were only four
thousand five hundred inhabitants. From the [Chicago] river to
the Desplaines River, eight miles, the whole prairie was often
under water. . . ."[7]

Channing became a pioneer by buying three parcels of land
for five hundred dollars. Although the land was carefully chosen
—he had the desirable combination of marsh, cropland, and
timber—he was hard put to make a living. He arrived in Illinois
at a time of financial panic and depressed economy. Only an
arduous effort would make the land pay for itself, and he had
little reason to work hard. Loneliness, he found, was inescapable:
since he had few neighbors (the nearest town was fourteen miles
away; Chicago, forty), the isolation was forbidding.[8] Instead of
freeing him to meditate and write as he had expected (and as
Thoreau was freed later by Walden Pond), Channing's frontier
life increased his restlessness. From early childhood he had
known periods of overwhelming isolation during which he felt
cut off from all human contact; and now life in a log cabin made
him even more lonely. He increasingly saw that frontier life
offered little for the imagination. Driven by his insecurity, he
made several trips to Boston; and finally, on October 22, 1840, he
sold his land (at a profit, the one successful business venture in
his long life) and moved to Cincinnati, the thriving intellectual
center of the Mississippi Valley. Here James Perkins, his uncle,
and William H. Channing, a cousin, were leading a group of
Unitarian intellectuals and radicals by publishing the *Western
Messenger* and preaching a frontier version of Transcendentalism.[9]

III   The Dial

In the same month as the move to Cincinnati, Channing's
poetry appeared for the first time in *The Dial*, a new journal
sponsored by Emerson and Margaret Fuller. In an essay titled

"New Poets," Emerson printed twelve of Channing's poems and offered with them a running commentary to "shade the abruptness & fragmentary character of several pieces & give them due perspective."[10] So, as he left his farm, Channing found himself firmly, if obscurely, established as a poet.

The years of idling, reading, and dreaming had prepared him well for his new career. His appearance in *The Dial* under Emerson's sponsorship ended the aimlessness in his life: he was now a poet, would be nothing but a poet. For a full year, this emergence as a professional poet had been slowly maturing. The previous autumn when he had departed for the West, Channing's friend from the Round Hill School, Samuel Gray Ward, had sent Emerson one of Channing's poems. Emerson, in his guarded, but enthusiastic reply, stated that he found "a sunny sweetness of thought & feeling which are high gifts; and the voluminous eloquence of his Spenserian stanza is by itself an indication of great skill & cunning."[11] Emerson complained, however, about the rough, careless composition that marred the verses; but he distinctly encouraged Ward to send him more of the poetry. By the end of the year, Emerson was ready to approach Channing with candor and encouragement.

In February, 1840, when Channing was despondent about his Illinois experiment and resigned to obscurity, he received the following letter from Emerson: "Your friend Samuel G. Ward, whom though I have known but a little while I love much, has communicated to me a number of your poems which I have read & still read with great delight. I have seen no verses written in America that have such inward music, or that seem to me such authentic inspiration."[12] What praise for a young, struggling poet from a man already an idol to the youth of 1840! Channing had heard Emerson lecture in Boston, had probably read *Nature*, and certainly had respect for this man whose self-reliance was already both anathema and inspiration to New England.

Emerson also explained to Channing in his letter that a new journal was to be established precisely for the purpose of publishing obscure poets of "authentic inspiration." Emerson had long seen that poets of genuine ability and unconventional ideas had no audience in the American culture that thrived on sentimental, pious verse. The standard magazines and gift-book fare was simplistic and treacly. "My quarrel with our poets," he wrote

Channing, "is that they are secondary & mimetic. . . ."[13] *The Dial* would open its pages to another kind of poet, one whose meters might be jagged but whose mind was clear of conventional rubbish.

But Channing, with growing unpredictableness, waited four months before replying to Emerson's strong praise. By April, Emerson was beginning to despair of capturing his elusive poet. Writing to Margaret Fuller, he lamented, "I am as far as regards the journal, unhappy that no tidings come from W.E.C. Jr." But Emerson's principles were deeper than his impatience. "I had set my heart," he continued, "on bringing out that poetry as more new & more charactered than anything we are likely to have. I must still hope for it. I like his letter to you. It is of the same strain. The self-subsistency of a poet all willowy or opaline as it is, is not less wonderful or less affecting than that of Czars & generals."[14] Finally, in June, Emerson received Channing's permission to publish the verse on the condition of anonymity. The shy young man was unwilling to risk public ill-will in something so serious as poetry. Though the poems celebrate emotional responsiveness, the poet carefully kept a distance between his public and his private life. Already the need of a "mask" was becoming apparent in his reactions.

In getting the manuscript ready for print, Emerson found the poet's "self-subsistency" could be aggravating to an editor. When Channing rejected a series of editorial changes, Emerson fumed to Elizabeth Hoar, "cannot the spirit parse & spell?"[15] But such irritations were local and temporary: Channing became, in the next four years, the most frequent contributor to *The Dial;* and his career with Transcendentalism's most ambitious literary project validated Emerson's hope for the journal. Coming as it did at an emotional crisis in Channing's life, the journal gave the poet the opportunity to pursue his life's work with no apologies. Encouraged by Emerson and Margaret Fuller, and read by intelligent, sympathetic readers, Channing came during the *Dial* years to be a poet, to live the life of a poet, to devote his whole intellectual energy to writing. The journal had given him the opportunity to publish what he had written; its editors encouraged him to persevere.

His rejection of Boston's materialism and religious orthodoxy now had a positive focus. He had found a community of minds sympathetic to his values of emotional warmth and sensory delight. No longer was his life a series of negative gestures in which he only fled from that which he distrusted in Boston. Now, because of *The Dial*, Ellery Channing became a professional poet. Now the independence which had characterized his life at Harvard and his trip to Illinois had a concrete expression; he had entered the imaginative life of his culture.

IV *Ellen*

The satisfaction of finding a vocation did not wholly relieve the tensions driving Channing; he was still a lonely young man who had to make a living. *The Dial*, after all, was not a financial sinecure. When Channing finally moved to Cincinnati, he made a desultory, futile effort to study law with James Perkins; but he found a more congenial occupation in writing for a local newspaper, the Cincinnati *Gazette*. With this job and his allowance from his father, Channing had ample time to write his poems.

The previous October, on one of his trips to New England, Channing had come very close to expressing a love for Kate Sedgwick, an old friend in Lenox. Startled at his ardor, she had kept him at a distance and thereby had called up his volatile defensiveness. Always overly sensitive to a slight (either real or imagined), Channing had felt that she had encouraged his affections and then toyed with them. In haste, she wrote a note explaining her innocence only to receive a strangely cold, aloof response from Channing.[16] Such emotional elation and then depression characterized Channing at this period in his life. He was desperately seeking some relief from the loneliness he had so long felt, but he was so insecure in his affections that he could not free himself from the mask of indifference he presented to the public. In Cincinnati, however, he met Ellen Kilshaw Fuller, Margaret's beautiful, but consumptive, sister. Ellen had come to Cincinnati almost by accident on a trip to the West and South to try to recover her fragile, permanently impaired health. During the spring of 1841, she had gone from Louisville to New Orleans to visit friends and relatives. On her way home to Boston, she stopped in Cincinnati and found a friend in James Perkins, who proposed to hire her as a teacher in his new school.[17]

Ellen had been the pet of the Fuller family. While she had lacked the aggressiveness of her older sister, Ellen was more strikingly attractive than Margaret. Even though the family always referred to Ellen as "ideally pure" and sweet, the girl had a mind of her own and could be tart when the occasion demanded. (A Louisville friend confided in a letter that she was impossibly self-centered and vain.)[18] Like Channing, Ellen had been seeking emotional security and love. Her father had died; her mother was suffering under impossible burdens of responsibility; and her sister had been frustrated in her desire to go to Europe and to write at leisure.

Ellen had been in Cincinnati hardly a month when the news of her engagement to Ellery Channing startled the Channing and Fuller families. "An event has occurred," Margaret wrote Emerson, "which disturbs my plans and disturbs my mind, so that I do not yet know what I shall do. This is my sister Ellen's engagement to—Ellery Channing!!!"[19] The Fuller family generally was dismayed. Here, amid all the troubles thrown on the family at the death of Timothy Fuller, was the prospect of a marriage that had little hope for the future. Only through unstinting labor had Margaret been able to provide a living for Mrs. Fuller and the younger children. Now, after her sacrifice, Ellen seemed about to begin again the cycle of poverty and pain! Dr. Channing alone seemed tranquil, but the rest of Ellery's family was outraged. James Perkins (who had never thought very warmly of Channing; in fact, thought him insane) bitterly blamed "Emersonianism" for the whole affair.[20] But Channing had once more decided to march to his own drummer and leave the family to their rhythms.

The lovers, of course, saw nothing but their own love. "We are not rich in the world's goods," Channing wrote Margaret, "but I consider myself better off in the love of Ellen, than were I master of 10,000 a year." More importantly, for him, Ellen meant the end of the agonizing loneliness of his life: "I have found what I have longed for these twenty years—a home. Now may the floods beat, now may the winds rave, & the great sun himself be eclipsed, for I have found what I wished."[21]

Margaret guardedly welcomed him into the family by recalling how favorably Sam Ward had introduced Channing's name to her: "Thus have you been so far known to me that I feel little doubt how I shall feel towards you. You say you cannot promise me anything nor tell how any character shall affect you. I had not thought of this for, of a nature which the observer may call vain and presumptuous or affectionate and trustful at his pleasure, it never occurs to me that those I am inclined to love may not receive me till they themselves suggest it." Painfully aware of Ellen's future, Margaret stated that, "Should you prove the wise and faithful guardian of my sister's happiness; should you be the means of unfolding what is beautiful in her character . . . you will have conferred on me a benefit beyond requital, and only to be answered in prayers."[22]

Not only did the engagement bring Channing a wife to end his loneliness, but it also brought him contact with Margaret Fuller, one of the most intense, imaginative critics of her era. In her, Channing found a faithful reader, an honest critic, and a loving sister. She never forgave Channing the hardships and pain which he inflicted on Ellen, but she never ignored the pure delight of his verse, conversation, and letters that she came to prize so highly. This friendship between Ellery and Margaret was to be rivaled only by his with Emerson and Thoreau. The years were to bring these friendships to maturity, but with his marriage Channing was now forever bound to New England's literature.

Teeming with plans for the future, he and Ellen were married on September 24, 1841.[23] Should they return to Massachusetts at once and join the new experimental community at Brook Farm? Should they buy a small farm of their own and settle in rural bliss? Margaret sensibly counseled Channing to be patient, to arrange for privacy, and to keep in mind his need to write. Finally, the couple decided to stay in Cincinnati for a time, bought some furniture for their new home, and waited for Mrs. Fuller to join them. Channing seriously devoted himself to his job with the *Gazette*, though apparently the editor misused his labor by reneging on the promised salary of four hundred dollars.[24] Mrs. Fuller was relieved and delighted to find Channing cheerfully helping with domestic chores, doing the marketing, and promptly marshaling his energy as a dutiful husband. The rumors of his willful moodiness and nasty temper were evidently wrong or at least exaggerated.[25]

More importantly, Channing's hopes of love and affection were fulfilled. In the fall and following spring of his marriage year, he wrote steadily: poems and letters came with newly won ease. He carried on a lively correspondence with Margaret, with Sam Ward, and with Caroline Sturgis, another young friend from his

early life (she had been a rowing companion on the Artichoke
River during the post-Harvard interlude). To Margaret, he
presented a kaleidoscopic figure; he was by turns bathetic, witty,
serious, jesting, and enigmatic. "Why seal letters?" he burst out.
"If I were a Transcendentalist I could not seal a letter."[26] Goethe,
he found, was "too heavy a task for an idle man." Channing
found it hard "to search for his beauties, & hang over his un-
fathomable sagacities, like a fish-hawk over a shoal of mackerel,
waiting for them to jump out of the water."[27] When she politely
asked how his affairs were going, he postured: "Affairs—I have
none of them. I am not a person of affairs. I may wake up myself
some day, & find I have been doing something, but no one will
ever tell me of it. I have never yet had any one tell me I was
doing anything, either for myself, or others."[28]

In spite of the levity that pervades his letters, Channing showed
himself a careful, intelligent reader of his sister-in-law's writing.
"Allow me in conclusion to observe," he wrote in March, 1842,
"how much pleasure I have derived from your various letters &
criticisms. I would you had written some plain, common-place
stories about men & things. I think you are disposed to mysticism,
to Germanity; it may not be so. But do write some plain stories,
or inventions about the everyday. Goethe & Bettene [*sic*] are well
enough. I want to see Margaret Fuller herself—not Gunerode—
not others."[29]

Channing obviously recognized Margaret's tendency to assume
a public role behind which her private life was secluded. He was
all the more alive to this complexity in his sister-in-law because
he himself had been developing exactly the same protective
device for several years. Channing was deeply suspicious of
letting anyone past the erratic, clowning mask he created. He
deliberately cultivated a brusque harshness (rudeness, incivility,
some called it) and seeming indifference to life's pleasures so
that no one might see how deeply responsive to emotions and
ideas he truly was. Even to his closest friends and to those whom
he most respected, Channing could be insufferable. Before his
marriage, he had successfully avoided meeting Emerson who had
deliberately sought to know him. In July, 1840, Emerson made a
special trip to meet Channing in Boston only to find him gone to
Illinois. "Having made one effort to see him," Emerson wrote
Margaret, "I am quite content to lose him, though I had set my

heart on an interview. But pen & ink are constant beside the inconstant wills of men & I have looked at his sonnets which have
not faded away."[30] The "inconstant will" was becoming a Channing trademark understood by few men. As he revealed his
emotional responses repeatedly in his poetry, he withdrew more
and more into the privacy of his mental life.

Emerson and Margaret soon had an opportunity to meet
Channing in person. As the summer of 1842 began, everyone was
ready for the newly wed couple to come home, and the lovers
were ready to go there. Channing went through a period of
intense homesickness and began to arrange for the publication of
a book of poems.[31] Reluctantly he left Ellen with her mother in
Ohio and went to New England to find a place to live. When
Margaret arrived at Emerson's on August 17, she found Channing
entertaining the family and soon came to delight in the conversation and wit of her brother-in-law. The two weeks she spent with
Emerson and Channing were tiring but consistently stimulating.
Retiring to her journal in the evening, Margaret found that, although her nerves were too strained to write, the quality of the
conversation had been worth the hectic exhaustion.[32]

Resolved to help where ever she could, she wrote Sophia
Hawthorne, one of Salem's Peabody sisters who had recently
married the writer, and proposed that the Hawthornes share the
roomy Old Manse with the Channings—after all, since the newly
wedded couples knew and liked each other, they could join in
some mutually beneficial tenancy. Hawthorne, aghast at the
suggested invasion, wrote back a masterfully tactful, but precise,
refusal:

My conclusion is, that the comfort of both parties would be put in great
jeopardy. In saying this, I would not be understood to mean anything
against the social qualities of Mr. and Mrs. Channing,—my objection
being wholly independent of such considerations. Had it been proposed
to Adam and Eve to receive two angels into their Paradise, as *boarders*,
I doubt whether they would have been altogether pleased to consent.
Certain I am, that, whatever might be the tact and the sympathies of
the heavenly guests, the boundless freedom of Paradise would have at
once have become finite and limited by their presence.[33]

The Channings found lodging with Margaret in Cambridge, and
Ellen joined her husband. The winter passed easily with Chan-

ning frequently making the trip from Cambridge to Concord to walk and talk with Emerson and Thoreau, with whom he quickly and firmly became friends. Concord, he saw, was the only possible home for a poet. To be near Emerson was a necessity; to find imagination and sympathy was to break from his loneliness. In April, 1843, Channing moved to Concord where, though he was later to live in New York and New Bedford, he was to find his life's work, satisfaction, and stability. If anyone should have lived in Concord, it was Ellery Channing. Here the woods, ponds, and rivers of Middlesex County were endless enough for a lifetime of observation; here were Emerson and Thoreau whose minds colored and enriched any man sensitive enough to listen to them. Here was physical and intellectual room enough for a poet to be unconventional and moody. Here was home.

V   *The Poet*

Nor did Channing lack a welcome. Thoreau had gone to Staten Island when Ellery settled in Concord, but Emerson quickly found the poet to be a rare companion. "Sometimes this summer," he wrote Ward, "I have found a true delight in the wisdom of his talk, & have been very sensible that there was no literature in these days up to the mark of his criticism. . . . His writing is unworthy [of] him."[34] To Margaret, Emerson expressed deep gratitude for this new friendship: "Ellery has many values for me, or would have, if I were better & more social. But the virtues & shining gifts of men admonish us often that our ears & eyes are gross & heavy. And for his sake I wish I were younger & gladder for he is, I think, very susceptible of influence from such as he could love."[35]

Channing interlaced these Emersonian excursions with more leisurely days with Hawthorne, with whom he had a less intense, less intellectual friendship. The men spent hours drifting down the Concord River lazily smoking and swapping stories, but their companionship was reserved: Hawthorne distrusted Channing's hazy impressionism; Channing was put off by Hawthorne's lack of enthusiasm about nature. Channing looked for color and light in the woods; Hawthorne was content just to be away from the village. Of Channing, Hawthorne wrote ambivalently: "He is one of those queer and clever young men whom Mr. Emerson (that everlasting rejector of all that is, and seeker for he knows not

what) is continually picking up by way of a genius. . . . I like him
well enough, however. . . ."[36]

Bronson Alcott, who was pursuing a visionary ideal by establishing utopia at Fruitlands, caught Channing's attention. To
Margaret, Channing unleashed his brawling humor:

The last plan of the Vegetable Eaters, has crept out of existence, in
thin smoke, like as all the others. Alcott & Lane, joined with Greene &
Chase, were to buy a certain Sudburian farm. Alcott contributing two
full-grown brothers, turners in wood, there being a water-power on the
place,—Lane money. Greene & Chase money & all with Alcott posts in
railroad haste to—in New York, unpronounceable town, where wood-
turning brothers spin, but coming back find Greene & Chase exploded,
having drawn back into their uncominatory testaceousness. Now, some
notion of buying the Manse capers in their airy sconces, to be met by
some other light dancing fancy & the two locking arms presently dis-
appear into gaseous fixtures.[37]

Channing's life as a poet received a large boost when Ward, at
his own expense, arranged to have a volume of his friend's poems
published. *Poems* appeared early in the summer of 1843 but made
little impression on the reading public. Edgar Allan Poe gave the
volume a scathing review, but Emerson and Thoreau recom-
mended it to their friends.[38] True poetry, after all, spoke to few
men. Who, in a world dominated by the counting house of New
York and Boston, could be open to such verses as sprang from a
genuine love of nature? For the time being, Channing was content with the praise of a select few whose taste he thought
superior to that of the Boston elite.

But these halcyon days gave way to a persistent poverty.
Ellen opened an elementary school, but her tuition was meager
and her students few. Even this timid step ended when, already
taxed physically, she became pregnant. When Margaret Fuller
Channing was born on May 23, 1844, the Channings' lives were
further complicated with responsibilities. Marmie (as the child
was called) brought added expenses, added noise, added irritations. Channing was increasingly unable to ignore his financial
distress.[39]

After returning from a western trip, Margaret Fuller had published *Summer on the Lakes*, which attracted Horace Greeley's
attention. Needing a literary editor for his New York *Tribune*, he

offered the job to her; she accepted but persuaded him to hire Channing, too. When he arrived in New York in late autumn of 1844 (before Margaret arrived), Channing found Greeley exhausted from his campaign efforts for Henry Clay, the Whig presidential nominee. Greeley gave some general instructions to Channing and left him to work alone.[40] Although he survived this beginning, Channing never liked his work because he had only the routine office chores of clipping stories from exchange papers and of running errands. Margaret, who saw him on occasion, did what she could to help him; once she even acted as an intermediary between him and Ward, who, too, was trying to help. "I gave him the money in a way you would have approved," she wrote Ward. "I saw he needed it, as he probably as yet gets none for his work. I assure you he was touched to the heart. A beautiful light fell across his features."[41]

In New York City, Margaret flourished but Channing withered. He thoroughly detested his work and found little satisfaction in the city. From the depths of his loneliness, he wrote Emerson: "Not only have I nothing to say, but I cannot imagine how anyone ever had. At remote distances from where I am, some faint possibilities of life in a shaded background seem to arise. Fled, O fled forever, are you, early and mysterious lights that surround the initials of existence. . . ."[42] The old specter of loneliness haunted him. Life had grown grimmer lately, but he found separation from Ellen intolerable. He hated the noise and confusion of the small house in Concord, but to be alone was impossible. This tension between love and pain came more and more to ensnare the Channings. He gloried in his friendships and in the Concord countryside, but this satisfaction was balanced against the harsh poverty that Ellen had to suffer. Finally, he parted with Greeley in March, 1845, and went home. Still without work, Channing helped Thoreau raise the beams of a cabin at Walden and even slept in the hut for a few nights. Channing continued to visit his friend at the pond during Thoreau's stay; he was the poet of "Winter Visitors" who came and made the hut ring with laughter.[43]

Then, in 1846 when Ellen was again pregnant, Channing suddenly decided to see Europe. "He thinks it indispensable," Emerson wrote Ward, "that he should see buildings, & pictures, & mountains, & peasantries, part of his poetic education—never was poet who did not see them—that he has seen this country through —there is no hope for him but in the excitement of that."[44] Ignoring his sick wife—though apparently with her approval; she knew how morose and angry he could be at home, so she was increasingly reluctant to oppose his whims—he scouted for the necessary money among friends, acquaintances, former schoolmates, and anyone he thought sympathetic to poor poets. When he wrote Henry Bellows, whom he had known at Round Hill School but had not since seen, he ended the letter with a demand for a quick reply: "As it is my purpose to sail if possible March 1st, an immediate answer if convenient, is requested."[45] Bellows, not surprisingly, refused to promote Channing's education.

But friends and relatives, as usual, came to his rescue. John Cushing gave one hundred of the needed three hundred dollars; Caroline Sturgis and Emerson each donated seventy-five; and the ever faithful Ward completed the account with fifty.[46] One bright morning in March, 1846, Channing loaded a trunk on a wheelbarrow and trudged down the dusty Concord street declaring he was off for Rome. Leaving his wife and child, he sailed on March 3; but, with characteristic whimsicality, he returned after only sixteen days in Rome.[47] After all the efforts of his friends and the sacrifice of his family, Channing could find nothing in Europe. For him, Rome proved no more stimulating than Boston, Cincinnati, or New York. He needed neither urban tumult nor a sense of the past to inspire him. Whenever he left the congenial Concord landscape, the springs of his poetry dried up. Though he soon wrote Conversations in Rome, his trip produced little poetry.

The importance of New England remained with Channing throughout his life. His inspiration as a poet grew from a deeply felt reaction to local sights and people; he was a poet of local effects. For him, it was New England or silence. As we will see, tranquility was an overwhelming theme in his verse; emotional harmony was an ideal he consistently explored. The urban experiences showed him how out of harmony he was with city values and manners. Finally, he came to celebrate a pastoral idealism.

The frustrations of his New York and Rome adventures can best be seen in contrast to the fortunes of Margaret Fuller from 1844 to 1846. She, too, had gone to New York and Rome to be a poet and journalist. Writing reviews and essays, she actively attacked the social problems of her world. She visited prisons and wrote of penal reform; she invigorated the feminist movement and made America aware of European literature; she went to Europe to be shown what the traditional, sophisticated European culture offered; she stayed to fight in a revolution and to record the passions which were destroying centuries of tradition. In her, restlessness and intensity were bridled by self-control. She directed her energy toward literary productivity; Channing was only aimless and inconclusive. In New York, she had earned literary recognition and had been the center of an intellectual and social group; he remained obscure and lonely, occupying only the fringes of friendship with a few men. For Margaret, Europe provided new stimulation; for Channing, it brought only disappointment.

When Channing rejoined his family (enlarged now by the birth of Caroline on April 13[48]), he settled with relief into his familiar world. He visited Hawthorne, who was now living in Salem, took long walks with Emerson and Thoreau, and gathered together poems for a second volume. James Munroe published *Poems: Second Series* in December, 1846, at the time he published a volume of Emerson's poetry; for Emerson had backed Channing's book and won from Munroe the same financial terms.[49] Like the first, Channing's second book was stillborn. The sales were small; the critical notice fleeting and hostile. Already despondent by the popular rejection of his book, Channing felt thwarted by Munroe's indifference. Months later (after his third book, *The Woodman,* had been printed) Channing wrote: "There are two other works of mine, in your hands. Of these, I have received from you a verbal account in which I think you say, you had then sold '*one copy*.' "[50]

In his discouragement, Channing turned to the company of his Concord friends. The woods brought relief from the frustrations of his home. Ellen was weak, irritable, and impatient with her moody husband. The growing pressure was released only with his friends; for, as he became less happy at home, he was more content with his companions. Emerson, always Channing's enthusiastic champion, saw clearly that the young man enriched an ordinary walk: "He is & remains the best company," Emerson wrote, "is always superior & inexplicable, and I at least cannot listen to his grave & gay sense without believing that one who overlooks men & things so unerringly, must one day report his opinions as masterly."[51] By 1847, Channing's place in the Concord group was secure. Even Bronson Alcott—long the butt of Channing's harshest humor—became his good friend; and the two eccentrics took walks, discussed beauty, art, and nature.

Neither man was blind to the other's weakness, but common ideals submerged mutual reservations. Alcott, for instance, responded to Channing's remarks on a natural scene: "Walked to Walden with Channing. He admired the clear serene blue of the sky which, amidst the falling snowflakes, was almost as hazy as the summer heavens. The clouds piled above Wachusett in the west were magnificent, and some lying in buried repose about its base were worthy of the pencil of Rembrandt. Altogether, our walk and conversation . . . was lively and suggestive and memorable. We talked of art and the new pantheism."[52] Not only had they shared an enthusiasm for the outdoors, but Alcott was a fellow rebel against Boston's economic standards. Channing could smile at what he thought was the fatuousness of the vegetarian experiments (for fifty years Alcott ate neither meat nor eggs nor cheese nor butter) or at the dreamy reveries of Charles Lane, Alcott's close friend whose zealous plans wrecked the Fruitlands experiment; but he admired Alcott's tenacious refusal to submit to the materialism of the Perkins, Hoars, and Danas. The two had so much in common—poverty, stubbornness, devotion to an exalted ideal of beauty—that their friendship was lasting.

The frustrations of marriage and family seemed to wane by the close of the decade so that even with the birth of Walter, the third of Channing's children (on April 14, 1849),[53] some of the quiet stability of the early Concord days seemed to come again into the Channings' lives; but this felicity was soon shattered. Early in the summer of 1850, Margaret Fuller sailed for America with her husband, the destitute Count Ossoli, and their infant son. Burdened by the republican defeat in the Italian revolution of 1849 and by the ensuing quarrel with her husband's family, Margaret left Europe hoping to renew her career and to see her family again. But on July 19, off Fire Island, the Ossoli family drowned as their ship foundered and broke to pieces in a high sea. Grief-stricken, Channing joined Thoreau in directing the futile attempts to recover the bodies and Margaret's papers. For him, this death was an immense blow; for Margaret, more than a sympathetic relative, had been a perceptive critic and a faithful friend.[54]

From the early days in Ohio to the time when she had persuaded him to go to New York, she had encouraged his writing and shown by example what an imaginative mind might accomplish. Her admiration was tempered as Ellen's life grew harsher, but she had accepted Channing and offered him her faith when often he had little else to buoy his spirit.

In near poverty, the early years of the 1850's were stormy. Channing supplemented his father's small allowance with occasional sales of poems to newspapers or magazines, or he chopped wood for a week, but his income was meager. His letters and the comments of his friends record a struggle growing increasingly desperate. Late in 1851, Channing, who turned to the lecture circuit in desperation, composed a series of three talks on society; and he divided his topic into considerations of the past, the present, and the future.[55]

As usual, his friends helped by advertising his efforts and by giving him encouragement. On January 4, 1852, Emerson wrote Marston Watson, Channing's friend who was a prominent horticulturist, urging that the lectures be given in Plymouth: "One other person I should like to have engaged, if the enterprise goes on, namely, my friend Ellery Channing. But I dare not quite say that he has any lecture for your purpose, until I hear his lecture on 'The Future.' Both the others of his three I have heard, and though they are full of wit and criticism, or sarcasm all round the compass, he needs practice in pruning."[56] Throughout the spring, Channing roamed New England giving lectures where he could: Boston, Providence, Plymouth, Worcester, even in native Concord (a lecture which prompted Thoreau to write, "Perhaps the most original lecture I ever heard"[57]). But the lyceum was an uncertain vocation at best, and Channing went back to his poetry and his walks in the woods.

Life at home had become increasingly intolerable. Ellen was ill and pregnant; money was so scarce that Ward had to give Channing two hundred dollars to keep him from bankruptcy. On June 10, 1853, Giovanni Eugene Channing was born, and Ellen's small reserve of strength was taxed to the limit.[58] Emerson, seeing the growing crisis in Channing's life, tried to help by proposing that the poet write a book about the walks and talks of the three friends, Thoreau, Emerson, and Channing. Emerson offered his journals and promised to find a publisher for the book; but, even more generously, he offered to pay for the work himself. To everyone's surprise, Channing worked steadily. In July, Alcott wrote that he had seen part of the book and was delighted with its wit and sophistication. Promptly on October 1, Channing announced to Emerson the completion of "Country Walking."

No publisher appeared, but Channing anxiously demanded his money: "I should not allude to these details was not the state of my affairs the worst possible," he wrote Emerson. "Neither should I think it advisable for one literary man to buy *mss* from another was not one at the top of the hill & the other at the bottom. But either the fortunate must help the [un]fortunate or the last must go to the devil." [59] He got his one hundred dollars; but Channing had well-founded reservations about the book. He might be an erratic poet, but he was a sensible man:

Again, your Journals will get badly overhauled; for I shall not scruple to *use* of them what I can. There is one great difficulty,—if we come out flat-footed, and call our book "Country Walking" as you propose,— and then put in characters like yours and Alcott's and Thoreau's, etc. everyone will know, (victims and all,) who it is . . . Will this answer?

Again,—unless great skill is used, even if we give, another name, and call it "Walks in Addlebury," or "Musings on the Piddlededees," and the like,—the secret will out. Flat-footed *Country Walking* would hardly go.

Then, with his typical whimsy, Channing concluded, "However, it is all one to me. If you order the MS. I will put in the figures; and write as the artist did under his red cat 'This is a Lion.' "[60] The manuscript lay untouched for twenty years until Channing published it as a portion of Thoreau's biography.

Channing had now done all he could to break the cycle of poverty that had trapped him. Erratic as his efforts were, he was not insensitive to his wife and children. Certainly his moodiness was increasingly severe, but his wife's love was still a necessity in his complex emotional life. The family was approaching a crisis, and Channing stood helplessly by as disaster engulfed him.

VI *Separation and Death*

In September, 1853, Ellen canvassed members of the Fuller and Channing families about her legal rights should she decide to separate from her husband.[61] To Thomas Wentworth Higginson, to her brother Richard, and to Dr. Channing she sent appeals for advice, comfort, and help. Channing, she said, had become impossible: he ranted, he swore, he could not possibly live with the children. "In a happier more congenial union," she wrote Barbara Channing, "what was truly sweet & beautiful might have unfolded into the full flower; as it is, I am constantly thrown back upon myself. I must wait a fairer more beautiful estate to develop in fair proportion."[62] By November she had made her decision: she had to leave him. She sent the two girls to visit their grandmother Fuller, and she asked Higginson to take her and the babies home with him to Worcester. On November 18 he arrived, took Ellen and the children with the clothes she had packed, and left with no word to Channing who stayed in his room during the whole day. Because of the attitude common toward marriage in 1853, the act was staggering, but inescapable for Ellen, who could not tolerate Channing's outbursts. "I know well how long, and much you have feared to take this decisive step," wrote her mother, "lest some regret should arise from having left something undone, that ought to be done. Now I feel that this step could be no longer deferred, that the well being of the children made it imperative. . . ."[63]

The bright hopes of the young lovers in Cincinnati now seemed far in the past; the forebodings in Margaret's letters to her mother and to Emerson had been prophetic. Ill and exhausted, Ellen had her four children, her mother, and her loving Channing relatives; but Ellery seemed lost forever. Since drastic action was his only alternative, Channing first threatened court action to keep the children; wrote cold, demanding letters to Ellen; but finally, and probably with good cause, retreated into his lonely independence. The Fuller family and Higginson were determined to keep the Channings apart (Higginson even sank so low as to pay a Concord stationmaster to telegraph him should Channing board a westbound train!); they naturally found Channing emotionally unstable and felt the necessity to put him permanently out of Ellen's life. How foolish, Higginson thought, that she should surrender to the "magnetism of a personal passion"![64]

Although the neighborhood gossips described Channing's joy when Ellen left, her departure depressed him as nothing ever had before. He blessed the generosity of a neighbor who brought him some food and added: "period of unmitigated blues!"[65] In desperation, he turned to Thoreau for relief; and they rowed the rivers, walked the paths, and kept to their routine of outdoor observations. After one of these outings, Thoreau carefully described his friend:

In our walks, C. takes out his note-book sometimes and tries to write as I do, but all in vain. He soon puts it up again, or contents himself with scrawling some sketch of the landscape. Observing me still scribbling, he will say that he confines himself to the ideal, purely ideal remarks; he leaves the facts to me. Sometimes, too, he will say a little petulantly, "*I* am universal; I have nothing to do with the particular and definite." He is the moodiest person, perhaps, that I ever saw. As naturally whimsical as a cow is brindled, both in his tenderness and his roughness he belies himself. He can be incredibly selfish and unexpectedly generous. He is conceited, and yet there is in him far more than usual to ground conceit upon.[66]

This analysis goes precisely to the center of Channing's life as a writer and as a man, for he was a creature of paradoxes and contradictions that simultaneously ruined his life with Ellen and enlivened his writing by making him more intense in his search for satisfaction. Both selfish and generous, he was first attentive and then indifferent to his wife. A loving husband, he could ignore or shout at his family; a dedicated poet, he cared nothing for the "particular" which enriched the work of Thoreau and Emerson. His indifference to precision made his verse vague and sentimental, but his tenacity to his vocation gave him a unique place in American letters since no one else was so close to so many of the major writers of his generation. His admiration for nature and his love of poetry were forever meshed with his petulance and conceit; his merits were always tarnished by his indolence and caprice. Ellery Channing was a paradox of attenuated blessings.

More importantly, Channing illustrates the tensions inherent in the Transcendental Romanticism that flourished in America. With no use of "affairs" (as he once wrote Margaret), he could never escape them: man lives by many sources not the least of which is common support of a family. His idealism led him to pursue the life of a poet with an admirable tenacity, to put aside the siren call of middle-class conformity, but also to strangle the affection of wife and children. There seemed no possible balance between Romantic enthusiasm and duty for Channing. More impressionably responsive to values of emotional liveliness, natural beauty, and literary charm than most of his contemporaries, Channing lived under and never escaped the dangers of literally combining life and art. Here Transcendentalism came to life; here it showed its strengths and weaknesses simultaneously. Not even the vagaries of Jones Very or of Thoreau show so clearly, consistently, and suggestively the dynamics of a major branch of American Romanticism.

In his loneliness, Channing returned to Cincinnati and wrote wistful letters to Ellen.[67] When he returned to Concord, he found his life was still desolate. He had not been able to live with his family; he could not live without it. He had sought freedom from loneliness in 1841 by marriage; now, twelve years later, he was still looking for an escape from that same loneliness. Here was a sharp conflict between an ideal freedom to roam with his friends and a concrete responsibility to wife and children. No matter how wearisome the latter or how delightful the former, he could not ignore the tension. He had stormed, threatened, and ranted in 1853, but he was a tormented man. Always unsure of himself, always willing to hide behind a created indifference or brusqueness, Channing was easily wounded. Faced with the helplessness of a vocation that supported neither himself nor his family, but unable to surrender it for something hateful, he gave way to fury. But now—after months of loneliness, after having to suffer separation—he was calm, even cheerfully hopeful. Ellen, also lonely and unsure about the separation, relented to his pleas; she returned late in 1855 to her husband, thereby infuriating Higginson and her brothers.

After almost two years of separation, Channing had learned to bridle himself enough to become an assistant editor of the New Bedford *Mercury* after he had settled his family in Dorchester.[68] Ellen's letters to Wentworth and Mary Higginson that winter were full of family news and small talk, free of the depression and worry of her earlier letters. She was evidently happy—an unthinkable possibility to Higginson's small mind. Then, soon after the reunion, Ellen was pregnant for a fifth time. On June 15, 1856, Henry Channing (later renamed Edward) was born two months prematurely.[69]

Ellen went to Lowell to rest, then to Dr. Channing's. More than ill, she was dying, and the whole family could now see this harsh reality. Consumption, the scourge of New England, had finally drained her thirty-five years of weak resistance. On September 22, complaining of a pain in her side, she went to bed. Barbara Channing went with her: "Then I helped her up to bed," she wrote her sister Mary, "and she sat down on the edge, & began to struggle terribly for breath. I call'd father & we held her & gave her brandy & applied hot water to her chest—but soon she sank & died very gently at the last."[70] Ellen Kilshaw Fuller Channing was buried in Boston's Forest Hills Cemetery.

CHAPTER 2

Lonely Years

A FTER Ellen's death, Channing faced a bleak future. Although he was only thirty-nine, he had published three volumes of poetry and the prose *Conversations in Rome,* not to mention the dozens of poems in *The Dial.* Certainly the decision to be a poet had been productive (*Near Home* was to appear in two years; his desk was stuffed with poems—long, short, sketches, and narratives), but his work had brought neither recognition for quality nor fame. Poe, for instance, had derided the 1843 *Poems* and made savage sport of Channing's famous name: "There are a vast number of uninformed young persons prowling about our book-shops, who will be raw enough to buy, and even to read half through this pretty little book, (God preserve and forgive them!) mistaking it for the composition of another [i.e., Dr. William Ellery Channing]."[1] Francis Bowen, the orthodox pontiff of the *North American Review,* needed less wit to damn Channing: "His poetry is a feeble and diluted copy of Mr. Emerson's," he said, thereby horrifying his Whig audience.[2]

America clearly was unwilling to subsidize this poetry of nature and youthful exuberance, but Channing was self-reliant enough to go his own way. *The Wanderer* (edited by F. B. Sanborn) appeared in 1871; *Eliot,* in 1885; and *John Brown, and the Heroes of Harper's Ferry,* in 1886. Although *The Wanderer* sold out its small edition, Channing still lived in obscurity.

I "A Gnome yeclept Ellery Channing"

By 1856, the "essential" Ellery Channing, the poet, the friend, the man of letters, had been formed. Although his life was to be long, his character was now complete, and the contours of his work had been developed. Like his friends, he was a man obsessed with nature; for its beauty, its mystery, and its emotional

stimulation filled his long life with delight and awe. After a moon-
light boat ride, Thoreau wrote in his journal: "C. thought that
these few faint lights in the ever-lit sky, whose inconceivable distance was enhanced by a few downy wisps of cloud, surpassed
any scene that earth could show."³ Faint lights and wispy clouds:
these were the materials—insubstantial though they might appear
to skeptical, materially minded men—from which life was made
for Channing; these were the substance not only of poetry but of
man's deepest responses to the "not me." "Nobody," he once told
Wentworth Higginson, "has any knowledge of beauty; it's the
rarest thing. People all go along, just like dogs, without seeing
anything in nature. It separates you directly from men, if you care
anything about it; you are unsocial and puzzle them."⁴ Channing
was ready to be unsocial; he was willing to spend a lifetime trying
to learn what beauty was.

Boston did not know much about beauty, he found, nor did
Cambridge (or Rome or New York for that matter), so Channing
left the cities in disgust. He was one of the rootless young men
who were responding to a developing urban industrialism with
horror and disgust (the "true madmen of the nineteenth century"
he called himself and his young friends).⁵ Throughout his years in
Concord, he had searched for and written of a new Arcadia. More
thoroughly than even Emerson or Thoreau, Channing was frustrated by the dwindling of the pastoral ideal in American life.
"What a perfect desert is Boston," he wrote Marston Watson, "if
anyone could believe for a moment there was anybody in that
place with the most trifling thought it would be only because he
had never known an example."⁶ Such revulsion led Channing to a
pastoral ideal that put the city at a distance symbolically and led
him to idealize a rural solitude. "The people of cities are like stone
peaches," he continued to Watson, "and the country-folk like
peach-stones: the one all sweet colors and flattery on the outside
and within, lime, and the others crabbed and hard throughout
with a bitter kernel."⁷ Neither the city nor the village was attractive to his imagination, but at least his "country-folk" were honest
and free from deception.

Repeatedly, his most pungent writing denounces the cities and
the men who made and wallowed in them. To Thoreau, he said
with almost desperation, "There is a city of 130,000 people, and
not a chair in which I can sit."⁸ He could see that, when men were

deflected from their deepest instincts, they were cheapening themselves by their own hand. Utilitarian "use" it seemed to him, was indefensible. "Walk with Ellery," wrote Emerson in his journal, "who finds in nature, or man, that whatever is done for beauty or in sport is excellent: but the moment there is any use in it or any kind of talent, 'tis very bad and stupid. The fox sparrows and the blue snow-birds please him, and the water-cresses which we saw in the brook, but which, he said, were not in any botany."[9]

Frequently, this hatred of urban life and love of nature expressed itself in Channing through his humor. From the early days of his marriage, Concord saw him as a comic. Witty talk charmed his fellow writers, and his solid oaths tickled the rougher sort who lounged down by the river. Often this humor lost its strength and became posturing and clownish when he tried to be witty with his pen. Writing to Hawthorne, Channing railed at the climate of western Massachusetts by saying, "I am glad you have shortened your longitude, and evacuated that devilish institution of Spitzbergen,—that ice-plant of Sedgwicks, etc. Good God! to live permanently in Iceland! I know nothing of West Newton, and do not wish to know any more; but it is further south than the other,—a great advantage,—and you can sell Old Boreas, lusty railer, etc."[10] But this strained exaggeration was typical of only one type of Channing humor, for his walking companions heard another sort: controlled, imaginative, fleeting, and incessant. The painful contrast between the imaginative conversation and the stilted writing prompted Emerson to reflect: "he has approached sometimes the lightness and pungency of his talk, but not often."[11]

Nor was his wit all of the man: the other half of Channing was irascible, petty, and shockingly insecure. One evening, he startled Thoreau when he grabbed the poker and punched his own cat because she was purring too loudly.[12] So insecure was he that the slightest offense (imagined or real) would cause him to walk deliberately past a friend with no sign of recognition, only to resume the ordinarily polite bow or nod on the next meeting.[13] Any gathering of people was too formidable for him. Not only was Alcott intrigued with this shyness, but George Hoar recalled that, though Channing visited his sister Elizabeth frequently, he "rarely remained more than two or three minutes if he found anybody else in the room."[14] These eccentric habits made him queer to his townsmen, but his sincerity, wit, and kindness never disappeared completely. Margaret Fuller best described his complex psyche when she called him "a great Genius with a little wretched boy trotting beside him."[15]

The lack of confidence underlying these erratic habits and lonely withdrawals permeated Channing's work as well as his friendships. He longed for security and therefore created poetic visions of a pastoral land of contentment and sensory delight. Without, however, a firm belief in his own power, he never had the ironic questioning Leo Marx describes in *The Machine in the Garden* (1964), and so Channing's pastoral poetry came near to being sentimental rather than complex.[16] He felt himself victimized by Emerson's coolness when, in truth, he was prey to his own insecurity. To Elizabeth Hoar he described himself well by saying, "Born with an ardent nature, framed for affection, for gaiety, the creature of impulse, and the child of passion, under the unsparing hand of this terrible master, I have become like a statue, a machine, in which no part of myself is left."[17] The "terrible master" was Emerson, he thought; but, in truth, it was William Ellery Channing.

Hawthorne, recognizing the skittish, unpredictable habits that made Channing more at home in the woods than in Concord, called Channing a "gnome." The name fits because he was open to moments of depression that Umbriel himself would have admired. Throughout his life, his bleak fatalism persists in his letters, even during the days of his early marriage when his life was light and promising. He says to Ward: "[Life] is such an inscrutable mystery. . . . Why so much toil, so much care in this, to be rewarded far in another—why the care at all, to reside in the world. . . . Why should [we] be born to bring down upon ourselves what we should choose of all things to avoid? This were to be born for worse than nothing—for self-injury."[18] Unlike Emerson and Thoreau, Channing seldom probed causes and metaphysical questions. For him, the presence of nature and beauty were material enough for a poet. Late in his life, he said to Marston Watson, "It is not for us, frail nothings of a day to say or to inquire ever so faintly, how that providence which works in a mysterious way, ever really does work."[19] These times of depression contrast with the vigorous humor, and the frustration came in spite of nature's benevolence—but these contradictions gave Channing much of his energy. While this complexity antagonized many men, it was an aura of genius to others.

Not only were the Concord writers Channing's defenders, but men as diverse as Henry James, Sr., and Sam Ward were almost hypnotized by him. In 1860, James, by no means a man easily distracted by superficial gloss in those he met, described Channing as "so human and good, sweet as summer, and fragrant as pine woods." Comparing him with Hawthorne, James remarks that "[Channing] is more sophisticated than the other of course, but still he was kin; and I felt the world richer by two *men*, who had not yet lost themselves in mere members of society."[20] This Channing is presented from another perspective; he is not the temperamental husband, the obscure poet, or the sullen neighbor. Here are depths of personality and mind that persuade by their presence, that, uncaptured in print, one takes on faith. The word "genius" is the most common cliché of American Romanticism, but the term encompassed a strength of personality for which no other term was adequate. Sam Ward had no illusions about Channing's limitations. "From the earliest days of our intimacy," he wrote after Channing's death, "I became aware that while he was intensely sensitive as to what was due to him from others, he was color-blind as to any obligations to them on his part. He was born so. It was the crack that ruined his life, made him so solitary, and seriously impaired his work."[21] But, despite these limitations, he was a "genius" to Ward; he deserved not only special consideration and care but also money and praise.

The Fuller and Channing families had other views of their enigmatic relative. When Ellen died, both families were horrified to think of the children's living with their father. The infant was tiny and ill; the girls obviously needed a woman's care. To everyone's relief, however, Channing had no intention of keeping his children; he soon left them with his father, the genial, ever-present Dr. Channing, who arranged for their care and support. The grandfather alternately kept his grandchildren with him and sent them to relatives or close friends. Walter spent many years with his uncle Richard Fuller, Ellen's favorite brother; Henry, the infant, was entrusted to a South Abington shoemaker's family. Dr. Channing took a special interest in the baby and renamed him Edward Perkins in the futile hope of attracting a Channing or a Perkins bequest for him. In 1860, Dr. Channing took the child home with him to Boston where Edward remained until his entrance to Harvard in 1874.[22]

Ellery kept aloof from his family; he seldom saw the children (Edward recalled later having seen his father only once), but he wrote occasional letters to the older boys, giving them cordial advice and encouragement. He slipped into the comfortable, though slightly awkward, role of a genial bachelor uncle whose duty is fully discharged with brief letters of compliments and platitudes.[23]

II *Wanderings*

Now more than ever Channing wanted to turn to his friends, but this very longing heightened his capriciousness, and he began to suspect even Emerson of coolness: "If he knew all the hearts he has frozen," Channing wrote Elizabeth Hoar, "he might better read something on the fall of human hopes."[24] Yet Emerson's supposed indifference was a projection of Channing's depression. In this state of mind he had returned to New Bedford after Ellen's death and had begun again his editorial duties with the *Mercury*. Staying at a boardinghouse, he divided his time between the office and Daniel Ricketson's "shanty," a hut behind the stylish, comfortable Ricketson home. Ricketson, the son of an affluent and prominent New Bedford Quaker family, had read *Walden* when it first appeared and was so excited about it that he wrote the author. Thoreau went to New Bedford to lecture in 1854, met and liked Ricketson, and introduced him to Channing.[25]

This friendship was timely because it helped Channing fill his lonely New Bedford days. Ricketson was an intelligent, articulate man whose interests ranged through art, philosophy, and ethics. Yet, intense, nervous, and a hypochondriac, his emotions were much too fragile to endure Channing's caprices; he admired the poet, but found his moods unbearable. After the spring of 1857, Channing's fits of indifference toward Ricketson became more frequent and harder to explain. Eager to excuse wherever he could, Ricketson concluded that "the world is too hard for such men, and he suffers greatly therefrom."[26]

Channing always found journalism boring, so he quit his job at the *Mercury* in 1859, returned to Concord, and settled, never to leave. His homecoming was as abrupt and typical as his departure had been. Delighting in an aura of mystery, he often refused to tell his friends where he was living. When supposedly in New Bedford, Channing would appear at Thoreau's door. When Ricketson had bid him goodby for Concord, he would suddenly reappear at the shanty.[27] Alcott found an often-interrupted friendship renewed as suddenly as it had been ended. "After a long abstinence from me," he wrote, "Ellery Channing reappears at my door today, comes in, and talks on Emerson's position and the cost of it. Yet he shall unsay and most likely deny his words, next time he comes to see me."[28]

At this time, Alcott had perhaps the most balanced, accurate understanding of Channing during the period when he was most troubled. "In all my intercourse with C.," wrote Alcott, "I remember having angered him but once, and then by intimating the distinctions between a man and his moods, saying that I had known a mood once claiming to be a man, while it was but a mood and no more—a thought too personally impersonal to be mistaken by him or forgotten at once. He seems to have been arrested on the way to existence, caught by Fate at its portal, and held fast by some Caprice, so never getting free deliverance from the loins of the Nature he reverences into the proper world of love and humanity."[29] Alcott's reflection is richly accurate and full of understanding. If often dreamy and woolly minded as a philosopher, Alcott was a shrewd, concise, trustworthy judge of character. Channing's confusion of the "mood" and the "man" was compulsive as he tried to make a momentary emotion into a permanent attitude. When lonely, he feigned indifference; when sincere, he appeared cynical. To their honor, Alcott, Emerson, and Thoreau disregarded the moods and waited for the man to appear. (Unlike Ellen, they could afford to wait.) Channing needed affection, but he drove off those who would be his friends by posing behind his moods. "Those who love me too well, I like not," he wrote Margaret Fuller: "those who love me not enough, I do not regard."[30] Once, Alcott defined for Emerson Channing's paradoxical relationships with his friends: "he had the keen appetite for society with extreme repulsion, so that it came to a kind of commerce of cats, love and hate, embrace and fighting."[31]

III *Thoreau's Death*

The friendship between Channing and Thoreau deserves a chapter of its own, but the story of Channing's life turns now to their relationship because he was most himself when he and Thoreau were together as they were now almost daily. They did, however, restrict themselves more closely to Concord than they had in their earlier wanderings. Only once did they return to their favorite Mount Monadnock in New Hampshire; they took only one trip to Cape Ann. Now they examined the local flowers, rowed the Assabet and Concord rivers, and sat in the rain watching the lakes. Their earlier trips had taken them on longer excursions: little more than a year after they had met, in the summer of 1844, the two had gone to the Catskill Mountains; in 1848, they had walked through the southern part of New Hampshire; in 1849, they had taken their first trip to Cape Cod. The following year found Channing and Thoreau in Canada; in 1852, they had climbed Monadnock together, then had returned to Cape Cod in 1855 and finally to Monadnock in 1860. There was little from Quebec to New York that the two had not paused together to examine.[32]

More than ever, Thoreau turned in these later years to a minute investigation of the natural world; Channing was still indifferent to "particulars." He saw little reason to revise his poems; he was too proud merely to imitate Thoreau, who was closely observing his world and finding ever firmer links between the particular and the general, between the concrete and the abstract. Channing stood strong in his love of the ideals of beauty, harmony, and truth; but he had trouble finding the imagery to organize and develop his responses.[33]

Channing could see that Thoreau's health was failing. The inevitability of his friend's death loomed larger and larger. Nothing in Channing's life—not the death of Margaret nor that of Ellen— was such a trial. For twenty years his life was intertwined with Thoreau's; and, sharing a devotion to nature and to art, they had depended on each other for encouragement and understanding. Thoreau had taken Channing on the simplest terms: he was a devoted friend. He did not ask Channing to be different, conventional, or consistent; he wanted to share that passion for truth he found in the natural world. Channing accurately says of Thoreau that "the living actual friendship and affection which makes time a reality, no one knew better. There was no affectation or hesitancy in his dealing with his friends."[34] This sympathy can hardly be overstated. Thoreau, for all his prickly independence, needed

Channing for an emotional support. Never one to suffer any fool gladly, he sought Channing's company, shared with him common articles of faith and common respect; and his trust was well-placed, for Channing understood his friend.

Channing spoke from his deepest experience when he said that Thoreau had "the old Roman belief that there is more in this life than applause and the best seat at the dinner-table." Thoreau had "moments to spare to thought and imagination, and to those who need you."[35] This phrase links three of the areas of experience shared by Thoreau and Channing: thought, imagination, and friendship. Channing knew that friendship was a part of life Thoreau prized; he knew his own life had been made lively and more complete by his friend. Less perceptive friends and most of the Concord townsmen were aggravated by Thoreau's abrasive wit, but Channing knew better. "His effects can all be produced by cork and sand," Channing told Emerson: "but the substance that produces them is god like and divine."[36]

In 1862, as Thoreau weakened, Channing visited him almost daily to describe the woods and to share his excitement about a newly discovered flower. Thoreau cheerfully responded to his friend's attempts to lighten his day. On May 5, Channing and Alcott together came to visit; the next evening Thoreau died at the age of forty-four.

Channing knew that Thoreau had been an immeasurable gift that America had so far ignored. Years later the strength of this conviction sharply impressed Emma Lazarus, a New York poetess, when she visited Concord. "Generally crabbed and reticent with strangers," she wrote of Channing, "he took a liking to me. The bond of our sympathy was my admiration for Thoreau, whose memory he actually worships. . . . I do not know whether I was most touched by the thought of the unique, lofty character that had inspired this depth and fervor of friendship, or by the pathetic constancy and pure affection of the poor, desolate old man before me, who tried to conceal his tenderness and sense of irremediable loss by a show of gruffness and philosophy."[37]

A few months after Thoreau's death, Channing began work on a series of projects to strengthen Thoreau's reputation. He wrote F. B. Sanborn (a friend of many years, a former Concord school teacher, and then editor of the Boston *Commonwealth*) in November, 1863, about a biography: "My plan is to prepare a sketch

of Mr. H.D.T.'s life,—perhaps to make a book of 300 pages. I am
very unwilling to ask your aid in this undertaking, but I cannot
see my way without aid. . . . That justice can be done to our
deceased brother by me, of course, is something I do not think
of. . . . My little sketch must only serve as a note, and advertise-
ment that such a man lived,—that he did brave work, which must
yet be given to the world."[38] This uncharacteristic modesty is not
at all false, for, about Thoreau, Channing held no illusions; he
knew his friend had a mind of staggering proportions. So secure
had he been in his friendship with Thoreau that he had no need
to hide behind his usual mask of bravado or buffoonery. As
Channing's prose indicates, Thoreau was increasingly a symbol
for Channing of how a life can be integrated and satisfying.

Sanborn, who had designs of becoming the "official" historian
of the Concord literary renaissance, agreed to help, encouraged
Channing to write, and began publishing the biography in December, 1863. However, after eight installments, Channing took
offense when Sanborn delayed a portion; and he withdrew the
remaining chapters. The complete biography remained unpublished for nine years until Roberts and Brothers printed it in
August, 1873.[39] When it was at last published, Channing's book
had a mixed reception in Concord. Alcott praised it for "its exceeding picturesqueness and literary faithfulness. . . . It is the
tribute of a poet and a friend to poet and friend."[40] But Emerson
was exasperated when he saw that Channing had drawn heavily
on his unpublished journal manuscripts without bothering to ask
his permission. Sophia Thoreau was equally angry about the use
of Thoreau's journals. Their ire grew from Channing's inclusion
of a portion of the 1853 "Country Walking" manuscript, long forgotten, but still handy. When Roberts objected to the brevity of
the Thoreau biography, Channing had merely opened it at the
middle and inserted part of the older manuscript to expand the
current one (and thereby confirmed his original fears that Emerson was jealously hovering over his journals).[41]

While working on the biography, Channing joined Sophia in
1864 to edit two posthumous collections of Thoreau's writing, *The
Maine Woods* and *Cape Cod*. Although both books were marred
by inaccuracies and careless editing, in 1864 they made necessary
inroads on Thoreau's obscurity. Channing's efforts to edit the
writings ended in 1878 when he drew on the journals to prepare

"Days and Nights in Concord" for *Scribner's Monthly*. Channing had, without selfishness or hesitation, plunged himself into the task of keeping Thoreau alive for American readers. He had refused to work with Emerson when Margaret Fuller's *Memoirs* were being edited, but Thoreau called out his strongest efforts.[42]

IV   *Lonely Remnant*

The circle of Concord friends, so important to Channing, was further broken two years after Thoreau's death when Hawthorne died on May 19, 1864. Though the two had not been so intimate as Thoreau and Channing, the novelist's death was another diminution of the poet's life. Even Emerson, now sixty-four, was less of a companion; for his once active mind was now fading into confusion. Channing was still a welcome guest, but the long walks and sparkling conversations were things of the past. While Channing lived comfortably, if frugally, on a small family inheritance, he settled into a life which, during the 1870's, become increasingly that of a recluse. He devoted hours to reading indiscriminately in poetry, history, archeology, and fiction while amassing a library of more than five thousand volumes.[43]

This bookish withdrawal was a pathetic and ironic conclusion to Channing's life. As a youthful Romantic poet, he had been dedicated to the development of his individual personality; now, in his declining years, he could literally devote his whole attention to himself. But, unlike his life in the woods and on the rivers, isolation had little impact on his poetry. He had become the antithesis of Emerson's American scholar—a man thinking and acting, a man in nature responding to his original intuitions. His Emersonian individualism that had led him to write withered and faded; he merely grew older. The one exception to this withdrawal was his contributions to *The Journal of Speculative Philosophy*. Beginning in 1875, Channing contributed twenty-eight poems to this erudite journal edited by William T. Harris, chief of the St. Louis Hegelian philosophers. Alcott and Sanborn had become friends with Harris, and they arranged for Channing to contribute verse and filler material of quotations to the magazine.

Channing's familiar world eroded further with the deaths of his father in 1876, Emerson in 1882, and Alcott in 1888. Only Sanborn, a much younger man, remained. Sanborn had tried hard to raise Channing's reputation as a poet: he arranged for the publi-

cation of *The Wanderer*, chose with Channing's approval the
selections for *Poems of Sixty-Five Years*, and wrote frequent essays about Channing and mentioned him in others. This friendship, which lasted almost fifty years, was sealed when Channing
moved into the Sanborn home in 1891.

On Thanksgiving Day, 1901, Channing caught a severe cold
after being out in a gusty storm. The illness lingered into December, then grew worse. Through several stormy, raging days, he
weakened until he died in his sleep in the early morning of December 23. When his erratic, but teeming life of eighty-four years
came to a quiet close, few people knew Channing; his life of
seclusion had completed his isolation; he had outlived most of his
contemporaries. The funeral on December 26 was sparsely attended; the few mourners (including Channing's son Walter)
gathered in the Concord Unitarian church to hear Sanborn's
eulogy. Then Emerson's son and grandson helped Sanborn and
three other friends carry the coffin to Sleepy Hollow Cemetery,
where Ellery Channing was buried near his closest friends, Emerson and Thoreau.[44]

CHAPTER *3*

Prose

A LL of Channing's writing is autobiographical to some degree,
for he never wished, nor was he able, to divorce his experiences from his work. He consistently thought of his poetry and
prose as the products of his daily life and would have considered
a later ideal of "esthetic distance" to be stifling and artificial. But
his prose draws even more overtly on his experiences than does
the poetry. In his three longer prose pieces, Channing looks to his
own life and organizes some of the critical principles guiding his
career as a poet. An examination of this work shows more fully
the reasons why his poetry developed as it did.

In 1843, he began in *The Dial* a series of fictional letters, "The
Youth of the Poet and the Painter," which remained uncompleted
when the publication died in 1844. After his brief trip to Rome,
he wrote *Conversations in Rome* in 1847, and in 1873, he published the Thoreau biography. Like his poems, the prose is marred
by inadequate structures and stilted diction, but these three pieces
not only clarify Channing's values but show the attitudes toward
art that were taking hold in the 1840's. In the case of the Thoreau
biography, Channing made a serious contribution to understanding a major writer. Surprisingly, too, the prose shows an imaginative satire in Channing that he thought improper to poetry.

I *"The Youth of the Poet and the Painter"*

The letters Channing wrote for *The Dial* show him to be
quietly enjoying the serenity of his marriage. After the difficult
years from 1835 to 1841, he relaxed as a husband and looked back
at his uncertainties and loneliness with a calm detachment. The
letters emphasize his attitudes toward introspection and toward
the emotions; and they show how intensely he and his friends
needed one another's presence for encouragement at a time when

this kind of art and their style of living were not acceptable to the more conventional critics of Boston and Cambridge. Most obviously, the letters are accurate reflections of the letters, journals, and diaries that passed back and forth between Channing, Margaret Fuller, Caroline Sturgis, William Henry Channing, James Freeman Clarke, and even Emerson and Alcott through the 1840's.

These personages were convinced that they were beleaguered, and Channing catches well the uneasy, uncertain intellectual life they were making for themselves. Thus, not only are the letters Channing's own answer to the tensions he felt in his life, but they are the answer that his circle of friends was giving. He and they looked for sensory stimulation as the source of an emotional renewal, but Boston answered them with an insistence on tradition and reserve. The editors of *The North American Review* regarded them with horror; Channing and his friends found they could ignore the *Review*. The classes of Harvard taught rhetoric and Greek; the Concord writers looked at flowers and fished. What the older culture had, however, was an aggressive assurance that it was *right*. The younger generation was more defensive and less sure of just what it *did* believe, but it was unwaveringly determined to explore, to find new forms and new places to satisfy the harmony they needed between nature and man's inner life.

With deft choice, Channing has the letters begin at the moment of crisis he had faced at Harvard. Opening with the days immediately following the poet's abrupt departure from "Triflecut College," the letters contemplate the absurdity of a social system making possible such a school, the contrasting joy the poet finds at an isolated gristmill, the dismay of his family, and the earnest theorizing of his friends about art in America. These episodes spring directly from Channing's own days on the Artichoke River, for they follow closely the events of 1834–35. The tone of "The Youth of the Poet and the Painter" is good-humored and quiet. The letters lack any real bitterness or fear; they show how far Channing had come in accepting his life as a poet. Eight years after the fact, he could look on his decision with satisfaction. Whatever tensions and failures lay ahead were not prompted by a fear that he had made the wrong choice in 1835. What had been done was done well. The only question remaining was what was to be made of the freedom.

"The Youth of the Poet and the Painter" represents the introspective literature being written in Concord in the 1840's. Channing was showing how his friends were responding to the currents of self-reliance. Because "know thyself" could first mean only "reflect," Channing's painter says: "I am desirous to see my solitude in its true proportion, to know how much I can trust others, and how far depend on myself. If my efforts fail, when I seek to express my life, let me at least have the satisfaction of knowing the origin of my ill success."[1] This emphasis on the process of self-examination is placed above the success of the painter's art. Just as Channing would later in his poetry hold up an ideal of sensory delight, he exalts in these letters the power to understand one's self above all else. "Give me light," says the poet, "even if it be a torch, to brighten my errors."[2]

Without hesitation Channing turns in these letters to nature as the source of that "light." With the same insistence on a highly subjective point of view, the poet says: "We need some poets truly bred in nature, who have gone out, not to look at trees and sunsets, and put them into their note-books, but drawn by an inevitable necessity, to unburden their hearts, and confess their imperfections, before the stern beauty of the perfect."[3] To find human life reflected in nature is the continual emphasis in Channing's writing. Not merely to display visual harmony, but to see the emotional peace nature helped create—such was Channing's goal.

The letters from the poet to his friend are filled with rhapsodies prompted by the color and form of rural New England as demonstrations of what could happen to a man once he let himself become a part of the splendid world surrounding him. If the imagination is to be freed, then only through the use of nature can the poet succeed. From nature, the poet says to the painter, comes spontaneity: "I have no conception of any thing which has a right to be called poetry, unless it come living out of the poet's nature, like the stream gushing from the rock, free and clear. It demands life from the depths of character, and must be written necessarily."[4] Those "depths of character" remained hidden, Channing's young speakers show, so long as men looked to tradition or to material wealth for their happiness.

Because Channing so strongly pursued his idea of the "depth of character," he habitually concerned himself with the possible quality a life might have. We have seen how the role of a poet was obsessive with him; he depended strongly on searching his own actions for the "character" he felt should be uncovered. Much of his rebellion from family and church, from Harvard, and even from Emerson was a tenacious pursuit of his ideal. He often felt threatened because even friends could divert him from a consciously lived life. Perhaps, he thought, only Thoreau was successful, for only this friend had lived the imaginative life and had the "character" outlined in "The Youth of the Poet and the Painter."

Artificiality was thus a persistent fear running through the letters. "I am out of patience with the tameness of late poetry," Matthews Gray, a third young rebel writes to the painter: "it is a feeble imitation of what in its time was good, and suited the age, and I feel that we demand an actual feeling of nature, which poets have lost. Our social life does not admit us into the sanctuary of human nature."[5] This tension between nature and society never left Channing. No more than Thoreau could he conceive of either life or poetry thriving under the restrictions of urban life. The city wanted respect for tradition; the poet needs newness. The city demanded material reward for effort; Channing wanted only heightened emotional responses.

If he could have the ability to respond, his art was justified. Writing to the painter, the poet says, "I send some of my journal, as I promised. I know you will procure little from it, yet it will furnish some picture of the life I lead. It is not a record of what I do, but what I feel."[6] This recourse to subjective responsiveness was absolutely necessary for Channing. So long as poetry was an expression of feeling, he had no need for precision or intellectual toughness. The sentimentality inherent in such an idea of poetry was good, he thought, because he had found the world around him to be hostile to man's emotional life. He was so convinced that America denied the validity of human emotions that his life's writing was an attempt to celebrate the "inner life." To be exact and demanding, he thought, was to be stifling and diverting. Once, when the painter tries to capture the "genius" of Italian painting, he says: "I cannot detach and criticise by the piece; all this is done in every guide-book and new volume of travels. I will rather speak of art, of life, of myself, of what I see, of where I go. And you,—will imagine the rest."[7] Art announced feeling, and the viewer was to supply the imaginative coherence. If this esthetic ideal is a weak reed, it still is evidence of how alienated Channing (and his young contemporaries who found him an exciting poet) was from his culture.

When Channing turned in "The Youth of the Poet and the Painter" to the motivation for the arts, he had an understandable difficulty. Having rejected precision and critical speculation as esthetic principles, he is left with an all-encompassing abstraction, the "infinite." "[Painting] is not so nearly related to what we call the infinite, or what we better speak of as the un-named; poetry is the religion, painting is the religion carried out in fact. . . ."[8] In good Transcendental fashion, Channing's painter looks to an Idealism inherent in poetry; but, without any real dedication to man's divinity, that first of all Transcendental principles, he is less than successful in finding the center of poetry. Channing never achieves the religious experiences of his friends; his poetry is a product of his responsiveness to nature rather than to a motivating gnosticism.

Early in his career, Channing displays the most marked of the paradoxes which characterize his life. He was in many ways the most typical example of how Emerson's writing influenced a generation of younger people. Channing has all the enthusiasm, energy, willfulness, and love of nature that Emerson imparted, but he never accepted the Idealism of matter and spirit. Partly because of a natural reluctance to copy *anyone* (Emerson and Thoreau not excepted), partly because of an even more deeply rooted suspicion of all religious points of view, and partly because of his intense concern for emotions rather than ideas, Channing remained a contradiction: though an essential, illuminating member of America's Transcendentalists, he resisted the intellectual principle most common to his time and place. Rather than look to "spirit," he looked in his own psyche and to his friendships for his deepest satisfactions. For good reason do we find that finally his friendships, not his writing, most characterize him as a Transcendentalist; for good reason did he come only with a biography of Thoreau to objectify the successes of living he so wanted for his own life.

Of the several voices clamoring for expression in Channing, the comic role was most lively and irrepressible. His friends delighted in his verbal agility and wit; and, from the evidence of "The Youth of the Poet and the Painter," it is easy to see why they did: Channing could be gay and remarkably effective when he turned to satire. The pungent voice of Uncle Dick, a retired sailor, brought to "The Youth of the Poet and the Painter" this other side of Channing. Devoid of the sententious seriousness of the poet and painter, Uncle Dick is a merry, cynical satirist. With aggressive metaphors and unusual conciseness, Channing uses this voice to attack New England's solid, but repugnant, middle-class orientation. Of "Mr. Penny," the representative money manager, Uncle Dick says, "like many another country booby, [Penny] thinks he will lay out his savings, now in the bank, earning him his six percent., upon land, which every year will run him more than six percent. in debt."[9] One by one, the respectable professions are burlesqued through Channing's exaggerations. Lawyer Smealmin "is a dry, spare, plugged-looking creature, with more laws in his head than straws in a wheat-stack. He sits at an angle of forty-five degrees, and lives on apples and sour milk." Dr. Phosphorus "you will find a greasy demonstrator in a red jacket, cutting up the carcass of a refugee Frenchman, who died at the poor-house of starvation." Or, if a merchant's life is to be preferred, "The great art in being a merchant is, to look wise, and ride in a carriage."[10]

Only in Channing's prose and conversation did he give reign to this humor. Poetry, he thought, was dedicated to "Beauty," "Truth," and "Emotion"; and the harshness and cynicism of social satire was woefully out of place in such Olympian company. But the satire is often quite superior to the poetry because it evokes an imaginative language from Channing that is appropriate to the disgust he felt for the social world around him. The poet, for instance, recalls his life at college:

I found here no scholars whatever. Some young men, deficient in grace, were wearing out the elbows of their coats, in getting by heart some set lessons of some little text-books, and striving, which should commit them the most perfectly to memory. This perfection lay in the point of a tutor's pencil, and was at last decided on by the votes of a band of professors, who loved wine and puddings better than literature or art, and whose chief merit lay in keeping their feet dry.[11]

Such a description shows the scorn Channing had felt (as well as accurately describing Harvard in 1834), but it has a concreteness and vitality his poetry often lacks. The worn coats, pencil points, and puddings of the description convey carefully and thoroughly what Channing had felt about Harvard. But he consistently kept separate his satiric prose and his earnest poetry; and not a small part of his personal frustration stemmed from the contradiction that the genre he admired most was finally less successful for him than the one he deprecated.

"The Youth of the Poet and the Painter" re-creates the style of intellectual life common to Channing's contemporaries in the early 1840's. Emerson had especially encouraged such activity because, lacking any printed outlet (save the wobbly *Dial*), these young writers found in one another a sympathetic, intelligent audience. So they shared journals, wrote long, serious letters to each other, and came to find their conversation an important medium of sharing. Thus much of the life of the mind among Channing and his friends was fleeting—letters were burned, conversations went unrecorded—but they felt stronger, more mentally and emotionally alive for the exchanges. "The Youth of the Poet and the Painter" shows clearly that these writers longed greatly for a sense of "community." Like Channing, they felt separated from a larger world of the imagination; like him, they kept alive and shared a highly personal intellectual life. This sharing was an encouragement to keep writing though they felt shut off from a larger culture. The stronger of them—Emerson and Thoreau—were more independent, but each had a need for a lively intellectual audience; and each found it in the group of friends. As we will see more fully, Channing's friendship gave assurance to a group of very diverse writers. As each wrote more, the friendships grew; as the friendships flourished, the writing developed. These letters show a group passionately involved with art and its relationships to their individual lives; the letters are the collective autobiography of a group and give strength to the fact that Channing's life allows us to see how closely friendship and art were united among the Concord writers.

Such friendship grew increasingly important as the only possible environment for literature. "The rarest thing in this life is a true friend," says Uncle Dick in one of his serious moments in "The Youth of the Poet and the Painter." "Interest ties us mostly together, and our chains are made of bank-bills. The golden bracelets of love unite very few."[12] Channing's anguish here was shared by the other Concord writers, each of whom was busily making bracelets of his own. Channing described not only himself, but his contemporaries when Matthews Gray says: "[The poet] is one of a class of young persons, who have lately sprung into existence, as distinct from the youth of the last generation, as Italians from Icelanders,—the children of the new birth of the century. . . . They cannot unite themselves with sects or associations, for the centre of their creed consists in the disavowal of congregations, and they wander solitary and alone, the true madmen of this nineteenth century."[13] Such a comment shows how self-consciously Channing and his friends found themselves different from all in their sight. They had new values, new aspirations, new motives for writing. Alone, they found themselves needing one another for encouragement and affirmation.

This first excursion into prose brought Channing to see how dependent he was on his fellow writers and how fundamentally he was committed to his vocation as a poet. The principles he worked from—the insistence on emotional stimulation, the benevolence of a world of nature, the necessity to trust his impulses —are articulated in "The Youth of the Poet and the Painter" with such insistence and fullness as to reveal why his poetry was often sentimental, scornful of materialism, and always assured that man could renovate his life had he but enough courage. The letters embody the tensions the poet felt in facing the culture that shaped his personal life. Moreover, "The Youth of the Poet and the Painter" anticipates the concerns of both *Conversations in Rome* and *Thoreau: The Poet-Naturalist* because in the early work he was groping for a form that would embody his ideals. He came closer in the "conversations" of the next book, and he found at last the full symbol of his ideals in the biography of Henry Thoreau.

II Conversations in Rome

Channing kept the same combination of esthetic analysis and satire when he wrote *Conversations in Rome Between an Artist, a Catholic and a Critic.*

The form of conversation was Channing's attempt to capture the fresh articulateness of his conversations with his friends. He had seen that these contacts among the Concord writers were intellectually successful, and he strove for that success in his prose. The book is his attempt to re-create what commonly passed between the friends on their walks in Massachusetts. Then, too, Margaret Fuller and Alcott had made "conversations" into a public performance; the idea of intellectual dialogue was very much in the air in 1847.

Again he split his reactions into opposing voices representing what for him were important attitudes. The Catholic responds to the religious emotions stimulated by the Church; the artist has the ability to judge and appreciate the working of genius; the critic is a pugnacious, sharp-tongued cynic whose comments on Italian social life are witty and harsh. By using these three voices, Channing hoped to evolve a mature response to Italy and its art. Each voice is designed to balance the other views and to achieve a synthesis of emotive response, intellectual understanding, and social commentary. The device is unfortunately clumsy, however, so that the speeches are set-pieces rather than an organized whole. Each speaker is finally betrayed by the excessive application of his own point of view. Like Channing himself, each of his speakers becomes a victim of a particular mode of expression.

Religion dominates the Catholic: he is an apologist for the Church's tolerating no objection to Roman traditions or forms, no matter how stultifying or meaningless they might be. Of the inevitable visit to the Coliseum, he says: "When I looked down from the sinking Arches upon the silent arena, once flowing with the crimson gore of the martyrs, and saw there the Holy Cross,— when a beggar-woman approached, and kissed this Cross, her little basket of gleanings from the litter of the streets put down— I felt how perfectly the Church had accepted the benevolent idea of its Founder, and fixed the holiest impressions in places where, otherwise, only the snake and the wild beast should have had their lair."[14] Every sight, every relic evokes a pious exclamation from this defender of the faith. Art must be sanctified; politics turn on the Pope's whim; the social hierarchy seems divinely ordained to him. And yet he is perceptive: his first view of Rome moves him to say, "I perceived, through the fading antiquity, a victory of man over his accidents. Above the mouldering skeleton of a departed nation sprang up the choicest products of modern Civilization."[15] This mental alertness is what Channing had been encouraged to develop by Emerson; it is the same ability to find new sights full of meaning that prompted his lyric poetry and that made him a conversationalist of extraordinary effect.

The artist, meanwhile, goes even further in his ability to respond. In many ways he is an ideal critic for Channing: self-possessed, he never presumes to dogmatize; open to the effect of a work, he insists it be understood in its setting. He argues strongly for an organic view of art: "I feel how superb is the cumulative talent laid out upon this fine art of Gardening. Nature has expended her resources in fashioning the surface of these gardens into pleasing forms. With how fine effect a little piece of antiquity . . . shows in a garden. . . ."[16] Each part of a whole can only be understood in its relationship to a larger effect; therefore, colors and forms please most when combined. Again as in "The Youth of the Poet and the Painter," Channing asks for a response to a unified experience rather than a questioning of what constitutes that experience.

The subjective standard of "feeling" again dominates Channing's esthetic point of view. In response to a painting, the artist says "In Domenichino, I perceive a thoughtful mind, wrestling with the difficulties of expression. He proclaims himself unvanquished, yet does not, like Raphael, glide with winged feet over the obstacles which embarrass the course of daring genius. Raphael parts the waves of expression, like a swift, sharp vessel under easy sail, that moves with immense rapidity, while Domenichino, with all his canvas spread, labors in the sea, through which he does at length triumphantly pass."[17] The terms of the movement which contrast the two painters are purely subjective. As the artist feels, so he thinks. Channing asks no more of him than that he examine his feelings, that he try to capture the intensity of that feeling. Like the poems, Channing's prose expresses his concern that the emotions be freed and expanded; for the same restlessness that drove him from Harvard is central to his esthetics. Only in the subjective test of emotional stimulation can a work be criticized. This view of art so permeated Channing's work that he came inevitably into the hypostasis of familiar abstractions. "Beauty" and "Order" exist in Channing's mind as entities whose existence is ignored by most people. A work of art is a testimonial to these realities; esthetic discussion recalls their existence to a dull audience.

But Channing's artist is careful in his eclectic standard of discrimination. Words must be understood, he often says, in the spirit in which they were produced. Of "Michel Angelo," he says, "It is not a cold repetition of a universal prophesy, that I see in the 'Last Judgment'; it is the rightful continuation of the same foresight into later times. This grand idea of an immortal life and a future allotment of absolute compensation to the departed soul, . . . appears in some form in every universal mind."[18] Although he refuses to relegate art to mere religious sentiment, as does the Catholic, the artist will not invoke a cynic's standard and disparage a work merely because it springs from a religious tradition. In this respect, Channing adds his voice to that of Margaret Fuller in calling for an honest recognition of the interplay between the uniqueness of a particular work of art and its historical, cultural context. Since each was trying to break the crude bounds of orthodox preconceptions about the moral function of art, Channing is intellectually quite close to his sister-in-law as a critic. Both his desire for emotion in art and his critical values agree with hers.

Through his poetry, Channing was increasingly interested in finding the relationship between a culture and its art. His narrative poetry especially (as we will see in Chapter 5) was an attempt to show how New England was congenial to the development of a unique poetry. *Conversations in Rome* announces this theme of a people and their art through the artist: "It is only when Art is brought into a nearer connection with the People, that we can hope to see the popular mind elevated, softened, and enlarged. . . . It is for the uncultivated that Art wishes to exhibit its best works. . . ."[19] Repeatedly he sees in Rome the interplay between the grandeur of architecture and the strength of spirit in the old Romans. Again, his abstractions intrude on a full understanding of the relationship, but Channing is firmly convinced that a people find their best attributes reflected in their art. Raphael "is essentially a Roman painter. . . . With surprising accuracy, he interprets the Roman character," says the artist.[20]

"Character" is less abstract and grand to Channing's critic. The world of Rome for him is marked by filth, pretense, and ill manners. While his friends become ecstatic about God and Art, the critic sees mundane Rome. He sees the streets, for example: "If, by chance, a hole is left open to let in the air,—what they call a *piazza*,—no matter how small, knee-deep in cauliflower-stumps, or banked in with filth and rubbish, there is your covey of loungers, or your one lounger. . . ."[21] He is appalled at the stench blanketing the city; he cannot escape the mud or garbage in the street. This vigorous description of the unpleasant scenes of urban life is matched by the critic's irreverent comments about the Church, whose splendor is a spectacle of incongruity: "the helpless Pope quiver[s] up the nave, the superb feather-fans behind, the triple crown on his head, the great robes of white; the Cardinals [dress] in lace and red." He sees "the effeminate troops, the rosy-cheeked English. . . ."[22] The Swiss Guards make a small zoo: "I enjoy the Swiss guards, imprisoned like finely painted squirrels in this cage of gilt wire."[23] "Uncle Dick" is loose in Rome rather than Boston.

The wit rescues *Conversations in Rome* from the tiresomeness of its esthetics; for, like Channing's own conversation and his satire in "The Youth of the Poet and the Painter," the critic depends on exaggeration for his effect; incongruity and overstatement are the recurring patterns. "There was plenty of the bad, violent singing," he says of a service in St. Peter's; "a Cardinal, and a great fumigation. How the deacons grinned when it came their turn to be smoked."[24] At one point, the artist picks up the comic role when he describes (with less violent exaggeration) the coming of the Pope along a street: "The Abbé began to hitch his robe and get ready, as they do; I pulled off my hat, and felt sheepish when along came the carriage. Down went the Abbé, down went I as well as I could for a muddy day and stiff knees; instead of the Abbé and myself taking a blessing, the Pope looked out of the opposite window and blessed some soldiers."[25] The scene is economical, witty, and evocative of the daily life along a Roman street in 1846.

But Channing is much more successful through the critic than through either the Catholic or the artist. Such a description as this one of a Roman tavern delights the reader: "There sits your old abbé, immensely fat, with a vast red face. Over against him is the group of talkers. In the centre is the pallid gentleman, in thin gray whiskers. As the fleshy person at the end of the table talks with that gesticulative force which no one but an Italian possesses, he cries '*Gia.*' There is the thin abbé, the smart young shopkeeper, who is saying what he thinks good things, the scarlet-pimply old man, who slouches his hat, and the big-headed dwarf. The fat abbé acts as moderator."[26] Channing is not always dazzled by art or longing for nature, and his good humor and wit could evoke a scene like this with care and effect. Not every New Englander of the many who were flocking to Rome was awed by the past. Channing responded to Rome's dignity, but he had an accurate eye for pretension and complacency.

In none of the three voices of *Conversations in Rome* does Channing finally succeed in establishing a manageable point of view. Though the critic sees and understands the social decay in Rome, he is too cynical to convince the reader of a genuine sympathy for the republican aspirations of the workers. The artist, though he is intelligent and thoughtful, never sees the social realities surrounding the works of art; he lives in a world divorced from the claims of hunger and filth. The Catholic is too sentimental to escape a servile adoration of the Church; his ability to respond with his emotions is too caught up in a blind obedience to dogma. Each man takes his strength (wit, esthetic sensibility, emotional responsiveness) to an extreme, and the reader sees the inevitable paralysis ensnaring each man. The form of the conversations simply did not allow Channing enough room to create a complex work of art from his various emotions and responses. Most certainly he had trouble expressing those ideas about which he felt most strongly until he came in the biography of Thoreau to find the symbol for a complex life well lived.

But the limitations dogging *Conversations in Rome* are not unique with Channing. Indeed, he is a representative example of the New England writers who were finding it hard to create the adequate forms they sought. Hawthorne was to come to the same impasse in 1860 when he wrote *The Marble Faun* whose leaden conversations on sculpture could be interchanged with those of *Conversations in Rome* with no violation to either book. Miriam's outburst to Kenyon in *The Marble Faun* is typical: "Sculpture has no longer a right to claim any place among living arts. It has wrought itself out, and come fairly to an end. There is never a new group now-a-days; never, even, so much as a new attitude. . . . A person familiar with the Vatican, the Uffizi Gallery, the Naples Gallery, and the Louvre, will at once refer any modern production to its antique prototype—which, moreover, had begun to get out of fashion, even in old Roman days."[27] Little in the way

of imagination or execution separates Hawthorne here from
Channing's idea of sculpture: "[Roman statues] seem stern,
large, powerful, and magnificent, but the exceeding polish, the
delicacy, the penetrating sentiment which belongs to modern
times, the result of a wide and reposing civilization, I could not
believe belonged to them."[28] Both New Englanders had trouble
getting beyond an abstract emptiness in their discussions of art;
neither found criticism workable dramatically.

Nor is the emotional turbulence of Channing's characters
unusual in 1847. Margaret Fuller, after reading Quatremere de
Quincy's life of Raphael, found herself rhapsodizing: "I went out
upon the lonely rock which commands so delicious a panoramic
view. A very mild breeze had sprung up after the extreme heat.
A sunset of the melting kind was succeeded by a perfectly clear
moonrise. Here I sat, and thought of Raphael. I was drawn high
up in the heaven of beauty, and the mists were dried from the
white plumes of contemplation."[29] Emotions counted for much in
Channing, Margaret Fuller, and their friends. When she wrote
tributes to Channing in her diary, when Emerson recalled the
witty conversations with him, they were showing how closely
Channing's intellectual assumptions matched theirs: he was
wholly a part of New England Romanticism in his attitudes and
values.

Emerson, for instance, surrendered to the same murky impressionism in his journal: "[Goethe] is the high priest of the age.
He is the truest of all writers. His books are all records of what has
been lived & his sentences & words seem to see."[30] But, unlike
Channing, he used this moment of response to go on to a careful
consideration of what the response meant. The result is an understanding of the relationship between the artist and his audience.
If art led to emotional stirring, it proceeded to clarification.
Emerson completed the process of mature creation, but Channing
was all too often content to stir the emotions and settle for
diffuseness.

Perhaps more than the other prose pieces, *Conversations in
Rome* shows the direction Channing's whole life took. His antag-
onism to his materialistic culture directed him to a very personal,
often sentimental form of poetry. That same tension made him
seek and form strong friendships with those who shared his ideals
most fully. Though this complex web of tensions harrowed his

family life, it gave form to and activated his imagination. He steadily kept to his ideal of living the life of a poet by writing, by talking with friends, and finally by finding in Thoreau his elusive symbol of the complete life.

III   Thoreau: The Poet-Naturalist

In Thoreau, Channing recognized all he admired and aspired to be in his own life and writing. The ideals of his earlier prose pieces found their living expression in his friend: a love of nature, a rejection of conventional habits of living, a devotion to man's inner resources, and a sincere affection for his friends. Qualified by years of close friendship and by an extensive intellectual sympathy, Channing was uncommonly fortified to write the biography, but the book was also his unconscious justification for his own life.

Although Channing knew Thoreau intimately and understood him thoroughly, he was not analytic in his book. His own life was too bound up with Thoreau's for him to be skeptical about anything in his friend. Concerned about Lowell's attack on Thoreau, fearing that he would always bear a reputation for misanthropic seclusion, Channing wrote an unabashed paean. He took care to show Thoreau's warmth; to combat the impression that *Walden* was a hermit's journal, Channing pictured him as an outgoing conversationalist; and, in doing so, he overstated the virtues in his friend: "No whim of coldness, no absorption of his time by public or private business, deprived those to whom he belonged of his kindness and affection. He was at the mercy of no caprice: of a reliable will and uncompromising sternness in his moral nature, he carried the same qualities into his relation with others. . . ."[31] Not only is this picture not completely accurate (Thoreau could indeed be cool and reserved even to Channing), it is contrived. Thoreau was a man, not a saint. But—ever prone to exaggeration—Channing distorts Thoreau's strength of constancy. Even at his most inspired, Channing fell prey to his own intensity.

In 1902, F. B. Sanborn revised the biography, added several paragraphs about Thoreau's early life that Channing had deleted from the manuscript, and published a new edition. In it, Sanborn identified the speakers of the conversational material Channing had taken from the 1853 "Country Walking" manuscript to make

Thoreau: The Poet-Naturalist longer. The later edition is a more ambitious work, but the earlier version reveals more about Channing as a biographer and about the state of Thoreau's reputation in 1873.

Channing had Thoreau's example of composition in mind when he drew so heavily on his friend's journals. In fact, the bulk of *Thoreau: The Poet-Naturalist* consists of passages from Thoreau himself, joined and expanded with Channing's comments. The biography thus had the virtue of printing a quantity of Thoreau's unpublished journal writing and the limitation of diffuseness because Channing could never achieve the tight organization that characterizes *Walden*. Channing was fully aware of Thoreau's skill in reworking his journal material. "The impression of the 'Week' and 'Walden,'" writes Channing, "is single, as of a living product; a perfectly jointed building, yet no more composite productions could be cited. . . . The materials were drawn from the utmost variety of resources, observations made years apart, so skillfully woven as to appear a seamless garment of thought."[32] Channing saw clearly that the journals made an extensive autobiography, so he was reluctant to obtrude himself into the narrative. Only a misplaced sense of modesty and an awkward handling of the journals marred the plan. Channing's own cogent and perceptive comments would have made a better frame of reference had they been more extensive.

Throughout *Thoreau: The Poet-Naturalist* runs the insistent theme that Thoreau had sought and found a style of life that allowed his values to mature and bear fruit. The habits of close observation and journal-keeping were not trivial to Channing; "No description can be given of the labor necessary for this undertaking [keeping a journal],—labor and time and perseverance."[33] He could see that this habitual care in Thoreau had allowed for meditation; it gave answers to questions; it protected Thoreau from shallowness and haste. If nature was rich with meaning, Thoreau's method of living would get at that revelation.

Thoreau's ability to find wonders "at your feet"[34] impressed Channing whose own poetry is consistently bent in the same direction. The biography captures Thoreau's concern with the relationship between common sights and extraordinary understandings. "Not one man in a million loses so few of the hours of life," Channing writes.[35] With as much patience as understanding, Thoreau moved from the most ordinary detail to a rich comprehension of this life. "The blaze of July and the zero of January came to him as wholesome experiences," says Channing. They were "the gifts of Nature, as he deemed them. He desired to improve every opportunity, to find a good in each moment, not choosing alone the blissful."[36]

Channing recognized the importance of sense experience to Thoreau. He saw in 1873 what Joel Porte has recently described as "Thoreau's intent: simple wonder—an attempt at continued amazement and ecstasy over the physical conditions of man's existence—without the Correspondential 'reference or inference' of which the other Transcendentalists were so fond."[37] Channing's own rejection of material comfort and his life-long responses to nature show him how successful Thoreau had been in living each moment fully. The biography reveals how Channing found Thoreau to be successful in living the life he himself had sought with only partial success. Channing thought Thoreau had created the virtues of man's possible life without having fallen prey to its liabilities. The intensity, responsiveness, and emotional fullness in Thoreau were living, graphic, continuous examples of how far a man could take his life. Channing describes what Thoreau had been, and what he himself wanted to be. Though Porte has tried to show major differences between Thoreau and Channing, this recognition on Channing's part of the importance of the senses makes him the Concord writer who was most sympathetic to that "insistence," as Porte calls it, "on the radical importance of joy that separated Thoreau so widely from his fellow Transcendentalists. . . ."[38] The young people of "The Youth of the Poet and the Painter" and the artist of *Conversations in Rome* had been visions of this ecstasy; Thoreau was the dramatic example of that possibility made incarnate.

"His fineness of perceiving, his delicacy of touch, has rarely been surpassed with pen or pencil, a fineness as unpremeditated as successful. For him the trout glances like a film from side to side and under the bank. The pitch oozing from pine logs is one of the beautiful accidents that attend on man's works, instead of a defilement."[39] Channing perceptively had seen Thoreau live the emotions of joy, wonder, and love. He was a living example of man's capacity to have an emotional life of variety and fullness. Channing could see in Thoreau nature's effects on a personality constituted to respond. Without reservation, Channing believes that all men can finally live as Thoreau had.

Channing understands not only the depths of Thoreau's emotions but also their significance because he was equally astute in seeing the inseparable connection between the style of Thoreau's living and his love of nature. The book's title is apt: Channing recognizes the connection between poetry and nature and sees what the combination finally meant to a full life. "He observed nature," Channing writes, "yet not for the sake of nature, but of man."[40] He knew Thoreau was not merely an amateur botanist; he knew that the intensity Thoreau brought to nature was finally directed toward understanding human life. Above all, Channing saw in Thoreau what he had found central to his own poetry: nature was the inevitable spring of all creativity. "His temperament is so moral," Channing says of Thoreau, "his least observation will breed a sermon, or a water-worn fish rear him to Indian heights of philosophy."[41] Channing had good reason to emphasize this connection, because he knew how extensively Thoreau had taken his study of nature into his intellectual and esthetic life. Channing repeatedly says that Thoreau had no interest in abstract metaphysics, but he shows how his friend had worked out an elaborate philosophy of living from his observation of nature. Thoreau had, in short, done exactly what Channing longed for— he made the full journey from emotional response to intellectual clarification. Thoreau's life had not been the dilettante's dabbling nor the hermit's isolation. He had deliberately found in nature the emotional and intellectual stimulation of creativity which in turn was embodied in a lifetime of writing. Knowing that Thoreau was responsive to all the moments of his consciousness, Channing naturally made him into his representative American. *Thoreau: The Poet-Naturalist* is a testament of faith in a full life.

As Channing read through the journals, he was deeply impressed with the necessity that had led his friend to write so consistently and the skill of the performance. His method of living and observing, Channing saw, "should have availed him little, if he had not been at the same time copiously endowed with the power of recording what he imbibed. His senses truly lived twice."[42] Channing could see how thoroughly Thoreau's writing had developed his personality. Far from being an ornament to living, writing had been for Thoreau the necessary culmination of living. "His sentences will bear study," writes Channing; "meanings not detected at the first glance, subtle hints which the writer himself may not have forseen, appear."[43] In Thoreau, Channing found subtlety and technique; he found ideas delivered by indirection. Thoreau always demanded of the reader an attention to the "philological" side of writing. At no point in *Thoreau: The Poet-Naturalist* does Channing suggest a shallow or superficial technique in Thoreau; he always takes care to present Thoreau's complexity. Compression had given Thoreau a style and depth not obtained by many of those contemporaries whose sentences fell behind Thoreau's penchant for the "concentrated and nutty,—sentences which suggest far more than they say, which have an atmosphere about them, which do not report an old, but make a new impression. . . ."[44]

Nor was Channing indifferent to the source of Thoreau's stylistic strength. He could see in his friend the use of figurative language, the transformation of the fact into the reality: "He saw the great in the little. . . . The hubs on birches are regular cones, as if they might be volcanoes in outline; and the small cranberries occupy some little valley a foot or two over, between two mountains of sphagnum. . . ."[45] These metaphors joining the common details of the landscape with large, grand images of nature showed, for Channing, how Thoreau's responsiveness to language allowed him to get beyond the limits of mundane description. Channing insisted on the importance of style to Thoreau: "These comparisons to him were realities, not sports of the pen: to elevate the so-called little into the great, with him, was genius."[46] Only an understanding of how Thoreau's mind worked would allow Channing this perceptiveness about his friend's language; for, if contemporaries in 1873 saw Thoreau as a cranky naturalist, Channing knew him as an artist. The "poet-naturalist" is not to be divided into one or the other qualities. Nature made the poet; the poet gave meaning to nature. If Channing himself never developed the imaginative language common to Emerson and Thoreau, he recognized it in his friend and accurately assessed its significance.

To Channing, Thoreau's ability as a writer made his life successful. Character, Channing said, may be tested by "whether the person lived a contented, joyous life, filled his hours agreeably, was useful in his way, and on the whole achieved his pur-

poses. . . ."⁴⁷ Thoreau, by this test, had an unmistakable character:
he lived consciously; he had self-possession; he wrote with care.
He had lived a life on which he and others could ground belief;
he had consciously held and tenaciously pursued ideals. He had
been able to feel the same tensions Channing felt between the
writer and his culture, but Thoreau had turned the frustration
into a rhapsody of man's infinite possibilities. In Thoreau, Channing found a reliance on self and a devotion to principle un-
equalled in lesser men. "To be faithful in few things," Channing
writes, "to possess your soul in peace and make the best use of
the one talent, is deemed an acceptable offering."⁴⁸ The moral
center to Thoreau's life was obvious to Channing: self-trust made
a love for nature creative. Genius in writing commended that
moral existence to mankind at large.

Erratic though Channing had been, he had tried to live just
such a life. That he failed in some respects to achieve his ideal
only added to Thoreau's attractiveness in his biographer's eyes.
The Thoreau of the biography is an ideal to Channing, for in him
he finds the rewards of emotional stimulation he sought in his
own experience and a full compensation for the turbulent experiences with his own family. His own lack of distinction was
made less painful if he could advance his ideals by strengthening
Thoreau's reputation. Channing's devotion to Thoreau is unquestionable—the friendship was as deep as it was long; but
Channing's unconscious motives were as compelling as the conscious. Thoreau had brought together all the elements of a rewarding life that had motivated Channing, and *Thoreau: The
Poet-Naturalist* was an honest attempt to present that life in all
of its attractiveness.

Channing could, of course, theoretically have written a more
complete biography; but, as so often in his writing, he insists on
an idealized version of experience. The same limitation that
dogged his portraits of New England and its people in his long,
narrative poems rose up in the biography to limit the effect it
might otherwise have had. Channing had an insatiable appetite
for exalted versions of human experience at the expense of complexity. He finally illustrates simultaneously the two sides of
Transcendentalism. The movement's weakest impulse was to
diffuse and rarify man's experience beyond all immediacy or
concreteness in its poetry and prose. At its extreme, it lost the

intellectual toughness it inherited from the Puritans. Channing's biography of Thoreau is a version of this Transcendental slackness, but the biography also shows the perceptive, tenacious man who best embodies Transcendentalism's self-reliance and its emotional and intellectual fulfillment.

Thoreau: The Poet-Naturalist is incomplete in its portrayal of Thoreau because Channing cannot see Thoreau's contradictions and ambiguities. He knew, but could not admit in print, that Thoreau could be as brusque as warm. Thoreau's distaste for social organization was extreme; his recognition of public responsibilities in writing came late in his career. His sexual life was incomplete and strangely passive. *Thoreau: The Poet-Naturalist* is too consistently a memoir of love to be a successful biography, but Thoreau's complexity was perhaps too close to Channing's own for the biographer to have the detachment necessary for a full understanding of his subject.

But Channing put the emphases in *Thoreau: The Poet-Naturalist* where they belong. Thoreau was a writer whose experience as a New Englander was made universal through a tenacity of will and an imaginative talent. The intellectual center of his writing is moral and ethical; Channing could not have been more accurate in his insistence on these qualities in Thoreau; therefore, what understanding and sympathy could do, Channing did. *Thoreau: The Poet-Naturalist* rightly assessed Thoreau's importance as a writer; it directed the reader's attention to his strengths; it kept alive Thoreau's name at a time when the whole of American Transcendentalism was passing into a murky twilight. Modern scholarship can pass by the biography because of the thorough, more ambitious works of Joseph Wood Krutch, Henry S. Canby, and Walter Harding, but in 1873, the first Thoreau biography made a refreshing way station on the road to a fuller understanding.

IV *The Prose Record*

Channing's prose reveals his life-long literary interests, and we find in it the rebellion from Boston's comforts, the premium on emotional responsiveness, and the love of nature that motivated his poetry. He thought of himself as a poet and devoted his whole mature life to poetic activity. Prose was for him an auxiliary activity for satire, and esthetic speculation, but the purest literature remained poetry. The prose reveals how fundamentally Channing concerned himself with human emotions and nature. *Thoreau: The Poet-Naturalist* glorifies their union in Thoreau's life; *Conversations in Rome* makes a claim for the success of Classical art in combining them; and "The Youth of the Poet and the Painter" pleads for an America responsive to man's emotional needs. With this consistent point of view, Channing wrote poetry designed to accomplish what Thoreau had done in prose. The success and failure of Channing's career as a poet sprang directly from this esthetic point of view as it was shaped and influenced by his particular personality: the ideal of being a poet enveloped his whole consciousness.

CHAPTER 4

The Paradoxical Muse

A man maturing during these years and forming close friendships with such people as Emerson, Alcott, and Margaret Fuller would of necessity write the kind of poetry that Channing wrote. In his youth, he was naturally susceptible to those influences which were rapidly changing not only New England but all of America's intellectual life. In 1836, the year Channing printed his first poem, Emerson's *Nature* appeared. George Ripley published his *Specimens* in 1838, the same year that heard Emerson's "Divinity School" address and saw Orestes Brownson begin the *Boston Quarterly Review*. In 1840, *The Dial* was started; the first Chardon Street convention met and shortly thereafter in 1841, Brook Farm was organized. These representative events marked the direction literature was moving in New England. Of such exhilaration was Channing's poetry born; for, though he had unique directions and responses shaped by his personal experiences, his work clearly shows what happened when a young mind felt the force of "Transcendental" fervor.

Those qualities most prominent in his life also left an impression on Channing's verse. Wracked with frustrations and insecurities, he glorifies emotional quietude in his writing. Rebelling from Boston, he turned to rural America for his poetic materials and repeatedly made his verses show a skeptical urban audience how their lives were being wasted. From the overwhelming presence of Emerson came the testaments to self-reliance and the affirmation of spirituality—though this last quality is partial and unproductive in Channing. Although he could not resist the temptation to indulge in a youthful melancholy, his poetry is most typically optimistic; for it reflects the refreshment he found possible once he freed himself from the traditions he associated with Boston. Only in his language, in the circumlocutions and in

the commonplace images, did Channing fail to respond to what
was best in his intellectual milieu.

The untitled sonnet, which closes his first volume of poems,
exemplifies the direction his writing was to take:

> I love the universe,—I love the joy
> Of every living thing. Be mine the sure
> Felicity, which ever shall endure;
> While passion whirls the madmen, as they toy,
>
> To hate, I would my simple being warm
> In the calm pouring sun; and in that pure
> And motionless silence, ever would employ
> My best true powers, without a thought's annoy.
>
> See and be glad! O high imperial race,
> Dwarfing the common altitude of strength,
> Learn that ye stand on an unshaken base;
>
> Your powers will carry you to any length.
> Up! earnestly feel the gentle sunset beams;
> Be glad in woods, o'er sands,—by marsh, or streams.[1]

In this poem, Channing, with a characteristic directness, announces his theme of joy. To be exhilarated, to escape the commonplace tiresomeness of life, should be man's goal. The simplicity of the sun and silence makes a satisfaction unknown to the
"madmen" who are embroiled in life's business. The apostrophe
in the sestet brings the sonnet to a triumphant close by invoking
the woods, sands, marsh, and streams. The optimistic tone affirms
the possibility of man's having this joy, and the very simplicity of
thought mirrors the insistence on the peace that Channing so
wanted. Like Thoreau, he gloried in the stimulation of the senses
—the poem reminds us of the pleas for sensory pleasure that fill
the prose writings—but Channing refuses to take his poem to a
point of metaphysical investigation. He celebrates a pleasure but
finds no transcendent reality in nature. While he shares close
relationships with Emerson and Thoreau, he is less willing than
they to find divinity in the world.

I *Limitations*

But this sonnet has limitations: its intellectual simplicity and its
awkward phrasing neutralize its virtues. Spontaneity is trapped

by convention; imagination is surprised by banality. Paradoxically, as Channing was glorifying a new freedom of the spirit, he was caught by the inadequacy of language. Nor should his shortcomings be ignored: he had a genuine accomplishment as a poet, but many forces were working in him, and he lacks the sustained triumph a reader reasonably demands. While these limitations should not obscure his achievements, they should be recognized for what they are. Even though his subject matter is drawn from the common sights in New England and even though his themes express an emotional satisfaction, his diction undercuts the poetry by being bookish, trite, or inappropriate. In "Hymn of the Earth," Channing makes the earth-spirit say: "My being in your Chorus finds / The echo of the spheral air."[2] The lines are obscure and imprecise; "spheral air" is hardly appropriate to express the poet's exuberance. Consistently in his poetry, eyes are "orbs," boats are "barks," fields are "verdant pastures." With few exceptions, the poems are characterized by such circumlocutions.

The tension combining intellectual freshness and poetic sterility can be seen in the long poem "New England" that opens Channing's second book of poems. Cataloguing the virtues of New England's honesty, thrift, industry, and tolerance, the speaker moves among the sights he finds satisfying:

> Vainly ye pine-woods rising on the height,
> Should lift your verdant boughs and cones aloft,
> Vainly ye winds should surge around in might,
> Or murmur o'er the meadow stanzas soft,
> To me should nothing yield or lake or croft,
> Had not the figures of the pleasant scene,
> Like trees and fields an innocent demean.[3]

Such poetry could hardly be farther removed from the American wilderness. Channing fails to convey the qualities of delight he found so attractive in New England because his language is wholly inappropriate and vague. The images of tree and breeze are too diffuse to capture any meaning. The poet's response comes to the reader divorced from any sense of immediacy. Typically, the language and the emotion are too widely separated because Channing maneuvers his poem into a self-defeating vagueness and awkward rusticity.

The stiff, inadequate diction came from Channing's belief that poetry was an ideal world to be insulated from the gross, harsh realities of daily life. The language, therefore, was to be "purified" and kept free of distracting crudities. Paradoxically, the poet of freedom and release wrote by using an obsolete convention of poetic diction. Channing thus resembles a faded Augustan; like Pope's contemporaries, he felt that poetry gained its nobility in direct proportion to its distance from daily life and the individualized experiences of living. All that was vulgar (in the strict sense) was inimical to poetry's "finer" sensibility. This concept unfortunately cheapened Channing's poetry because it was directly opposed to the poetry's themes. Exuberant life and "poetic" diction make an unhappy mixture.

This contradiction can be seen clearly when Channing's conversations with Emerson are contrasted with his writing. All his friends praised his verbal spontaneity, his quick-witted conversation. Thoreau and Emerson found that his presence released their own creativity because he was intelligent, perceptive, and verbally astute. "In walking with Ellery," Emerson said, "you shall always see what was never before shown to the eye of man."[4] Yet Channing deliberately rid his poetry of this imaginative responsiveness. Farming, he told Emerson, was "an attempt to outwit God with a hoe."[5] But, in his poetry, Channing traded the delightful figure of speech for a doleful banality: "Labor the song of praise, that sounds divine / And better than all sacred hymns of mine."[6] This contrast is no sport: Channing's verse deliberately renounces his most inventive genius; the paradox of his temperament rises again to thwart his best impulses. The same quirk that led him to love his wife yet sacrifice her feelings, that honored his friends but made them victims of his boorishness, frequently enervated his poetry. The paradoxes in his life and work are simultaneously the driving forces of his creativity and the destroyers of all he sought.

Recognizing this inner turbulence, he turned to poetry for release: "So may we our lives control, / Cast aside what we desire, / Feeling that the sweeping soul / Has than earthly path, a higher."[7] Since this higher path for Channing was poetry, he deliberately sought to live the life of a poet: removed from commerce, openly scornful of Boston and all it symbolized, delighting in personal responses to nature. In a period openly devoted to self-reliance, Channing felt that to *live* as a poet was more important than merely writing poetry. His attitudes, his daily habits, his eccentricities all helped him create a role. Nor was he alone in his conception of the poet's life. Emerson, throughout his essays, defines man's style of life as an outward symbol of an inner experience. To devote oneself to poetry showed a sympathy with imagination, joy, and love that Emerson found redemptive. "Here is poetry," he wrote introducing Channing in *The Dial*, "which asks no aid of magnitude or number, of blood or crime, but finds theatre enough in the first field or brookside, breadth and depth enough in the flow of its own thought. Here is self-repose, which to our mind is stabler than the Pyramids; here is self-respect which leads a man to date from his heart more proudly than from Rome."[8] Emerson, seeing the connection between the desire to write and the quality of Channing's life, emphasizes the quality of living rather than the practical consequences of a man's life. For this reason, Channing was closest to Thoreau, found in him his symbol of a complete life, and tried to make his own poetry into a means of having the satisfactions of a life well lived.

So the limitations that plagued Channing's poetry sprang directly out of his intense longing to make his work embody his own deepest emotional needs. Poetry was too "fine" so it suffered from an artificial decorum; emotional vitality was so important that Channing renounced the indirections and subtleties we expect and fell into a sentimental indulgence. But these short-comings are not the final basis of an estimate of Channing or his work. Despite these flaws, his poetry has strengths; for his rebellion from the city, his version of American pastoral idealism, and his veneration of beauty and self-reliance show us more clearly what were the tensions and possible responses facing American writers of the 1840's and 50's.

II *The City*

Nothing was more constant among these writers than their distrust of the materialism centered in urban life. As Leo Marx shows, the American ideal of a pastoral idyll found fertile ground among the Transcendentalists.[9] From Emerson's essays to Brook Farm, from Fouristic socialism to mystical intuition, the literary energy of New England in these years was directed against all that Boston symbolized. In "Reverence," Channing explores several reasons for man's loss of emotional satisfaction: "Men are foul, / With avarice, ambition and deceit." This loathsome trinity denies man's moral energy by blinding him to the possibility of true reverence. Echoing his own rebellion from his family, Channing concludes:

> The worst of all, ambition. This is life
> Spent in a feverish chase for selfish ends,
> Which has no virtue to redeem its toil
> But one long, stagnant hope to raise the self.
> The miser's life to this seems sweet and fair;
> Better to pile the glittering coin, than seek
> To overtop our brothers and our loves.[10]

The urban man has spent his life but has sacrificed his "virtue" in meaningless work. Both the "feverish chase" and the "selfish ends" stand for Channing as the typical realities of modern existence. The goals of such a life diminish man's humanity because any possibility of brotherhood dies in the vulgarity of greed and the perversion of egotism. The city tempts man to satisfy his greed at the expense of his human feelings. Separated from his fellows, he is isolated in a self-defeating, materialistic world.

A later, untitled, sonnet shows Channing's despair at the futile energy of such a life:

> An endless round of formless circumstance
> The unthinking men go treading day by day,
> As in the sparkling sunbeams the motes play,
> And, like the busy crowd, keep timeless dance.[11]

The "timeless dance" catches precisely Channing's disgust with meaningless activity: movement without grace vulgarizes life. He heightens his disgust by contrasting the bright, free dust motes (whose natural motion is delightful, whose activity is directed to no "gain") with the disarraying wind of commerce. The inevitable end of urban life, he saw, had been the loss of delight. New England had shifted from a life in which work could ennoble man's living to an existence dominated by tedium. "Work is monotonous, a war for wealth," he wrote. "The universe is plainly out of health."[12] If man could but recover delight in work

for its own sake, if he could but be free from "things," something
approaching health could be recovered.

Reflecting on New England's rapid change from a rural to an
urban society, he wrote in "New England." The poem opening
his second book:

> They do malign us who contract our hope
> To prudent gain or blind religious zeal,
> More signs than these shine in our horoscope,
> Nobly to live, to do, and dare, and feel,
> Knit to each other by firm bands of steel,
> Our eyes to God we turn, our hearts to home,
> Standing content beneath the azure dome.[13]

"Prudent gain" might do for the wise and good of Boston, but for
a man who wants a richer life, such a contraction of human
possibility was intolerable. Confronted with this reduction of life,
Channing expresses his frustration through his images of sickness,
restriction, and tedium. Commercial, urban living threatened to
become an absolute norm for America. His horror in these poems
is so fundamental that his work inevitably focused on man's
emotions, on nature, and on a willful control of life.

Channing's reaction is a variant of the "cultural primitivism"
described by A. O. Lovejoy as "the conviction that the time—
whatever time may, for a given writer, be in question—is out of
joint; that what is wrong with it is due to an abnormal complexity
and sophistication in the life of civilized man, to the pathological
multiplicity and emulativeness of his desires and the oppressive
overabundance of his belongings, and to the factitiousness and
want of inner spontaneity of his emotions. . . ."[14] Lovejoy's
emphasis on frustration is particularly apt because Channing lived
a life of rebellion that, despite its successes, was never free from
a sense of failure. The city was the reality and the image that
affected him deeply from his youth to his death. His life symbolically spanned the growth of Boston from a moderately lazy, far
from vibrant seaport in 1817, to a fully developed twentieth-
century city in 1901. Sanborn remarks that Channing's earliest
memories of Boston were of a quiet town where one could still
keep a goat or cow in relative simplicity;[15] but by 1835, when he
left Harvard, Boston was already a metropolis to be feared with

an inchoate distrust. Leo Marx's study, *The Machine in the Garden*, calls this generalized hostility a "sentimental pastoralism" that is widely felt in American culture. What Channing strove for was the making of this sentimental pastoral impulse into literature. He sought the "complex" pastoralism described by Marx as a use of symbolic language to express a complex attitude toward nature.[16] As we will see, Marx's description of American pastoralism is most useful in discussing Channing's later narrative poems; but *The Machine in the Garden* provides one accurate point of reference in seeing how Channing approached nature in his poetry.

Beginning with the image of the "garden," Marx demonstrates how pervasive and deeply held has been the idea of the "new land" in American culture. He shows how Virgil's first *Eclogue* set the patterns of a "middle landscape" where the shepherd has withdrawn from the city but has stopped short of fleeing to a primitive wilderness. This "pastoral idea," says Marx, "is an embodiment of what Lovejoy calls 'semi-primitivism'; it is located in a middle ground somewhere 'between,' yet in a transcendent relation to, the opposing forces of civilization and nature."[17] This idea of a "middle ground" is central to Marx's analysis, for this complex balance between the pure wilderness and the city allows for a complex irony to develop in American pastoralism, and this "middle ground" is the theater for the emerging "counterforce" that becomes the "machine" in the American garden.

This ideal of the "garden" had been maturing for almost two and a half centuries when Channing began his imaginative exploration of nature. From the earliest travel books about America until well into the twentieth century, this image of the garden world has dominated how we and others look at American culture. Channing responded to this image, accepted the challenge of finding a better kind of life than that lived in Boston, and made nature the center of his poetry.

III *Nature*

As the story of his life has shown us, Channing early saw that nature was the source of emotional vitality. He marched to the same drummer that beat the rhythms for Emerson's *Nature*, Thoreau's *Walden*, and Whitman's *Leaves of Grass*. In an apos-

trophe to his readers, he poses the problem for which there was
no real answer:

> If I could say what landscape says,
> And human pictures say far more,
> If I could twine the sunny days
> With the rich colors on the floor
> Of daily Love, how thou and I
> Might be refreshed with charity.[18]

The poet's task is clear; his success, questionable. Though the
interpreter may be halting, the need is so commanding that only
a lifetime of effort will suffice. Channing set himself resolutely to
showing what landscapes were saying by interfusing color and
emotion. But nature never prompted the metaphysics and episte-
mology that led Emerson to question the world around him.
Channing asks few questions; he rests content in charting his
reactions and in championing a style of living geared to using
the best nature had to offer.

He finds, for instance, a moving force in the natural world; but
he seldom speculates on what that power might be or what its
implications are for man. In "October," a poem from *The Dial*,
Channing concludes by acknowledging a vague presence in the
colors and frosts of autumn:

> O find in every haze that shines
> A brief appearance without lines,
> A single word,—no finite joy;
>   For present is a Power
>   Which we may not annoy,
> Yet love him stronger every hour.[19]

The weakness of thought in this poem is not simple laziness nor
confusion. Repeatedly Channing recognized a force which he
could neither honestly call "God" (as the orthodox do) nor
"Oversoul" (as the Transcendentalists would): simply "Power"
came to be his term. A moving agent extended into man's perceptions, but the need to explore that causality never challenged
Channing's imagination.

His alternative is expressed in "The Earth Spirit," a poem he

often republished and one his friends thought especially re-
markable:

> I have woven shrouds of air
>   In a loom of hurrying light,
> For the trees which blossoms bear,
>   And gilded them with sheets of bright;
> I fall upon the grass like love's first kiss,
> I make the golden flies and their fine bliss.[20]

Here the images of light and color convey a creativity appropriate
to the "Earth Spirit," for through nature comes rejuvenation. The
exuberant tone and the welter of images show how excitedly
Channing responded to this "power" in nature. The fecundity
moved him to poetry; the visual delight mirrors his capability of
responding to the sumptuousness nature daily presents to man.
His poetry increasingly shows that his art was highly subjective,
for he had no ironic distance between himself and nature: the
"garden" was his private home.

Power, for instance could be awesome when embodied in the
mountains:

> What are ye, grand, unuttered words of Power,
> Why stand you thus, balancing only earth,
> Shall not an echo wake, an untold hour
> Stir in your cavernous breasts a giant birth, . . .[21]

The response here is simple: overwhelming nature makes power
concrete. Channing wants but to show the ability to respond to
nature. How appalling, he says, that man should live so as to
deaden his emotions. If no one looks at a mountain with responsiveness, then nature's awesomeness never penetrates man's
life. Such a poem assumes that routine commerce, urban herding,
and indifference thwart the possibilities of man's achieving a
more active engagement with his life.

Most commonly, he finds, man longs for the power of his
industrial creations rather than for the moving forces of nature.
Using the spring at Walden Pond, Channing draws an effective
contrast between the simple pleasure of drinking and the nauseous
demands of the railroad that had intruded on this spot of natural
delight. "Walden Spring" opens with an invocation to the pond

asking for the memory of delightful days. The poet recalls the spring "Dancing in yellow circles on the sand, / And carving through the ooze a crystal bowl." Refreshed, he relaxes and lets his imagination construct a scathing image of the railroad:

> And as I dreamed of these, I marked the roof,
> Then newly built above the placid spring,
> Resting upon some awkward masonry.
> In truth our village has become a butt
> For one of these fleet railroad shafts, and o'er
> Our peaceful plain, its soothing sound is—Concord,
> Four times and more each day a rumbling train
> Of painted cars rolls on the iron road,
> Prefigured in its advent by sharp screams
> That Pandemonium satisfied should hear.
> The steaming tug athirst, and lacking drink,
> The railroad eye, direct with fatal stroke
> Smote the spring's covert, and by leaden drain
> Thieved its cold crystal for the engine's breast
> Strange! that the playful current from the woods,
> Should drag the freighted train, chatting with fire,
> And point the tarnished rail with man and trade.[22]

The image of Concord reduced to a mere buttress for the railroad shaft captures the horror Channing felt in seeing the triumph of industrialism. The purity of the spring fades as the water makes the steam that powers the hellish uproar. The delicacy of the crystal and the delight of color are consumed in the awesome, ruinous power of the machine.

Channing has given in "Walden Spring" a complex version of that "counterforce" Marx describes. Throughout the pastoral tradition from Virgil onward, Marx says, the pastoral middle ground has been subject to an opposing view of reality. The pastoral is an idyll; the counterforce is the "more real" world which takes into account those forces that work against the idyll.[23] Increasingly, our culture has come to project images of the machine as the American challenge to a simple pastoral dream. But, as Marx so effectively shows, this intrusion of the machine into our garden was more than symbolic, for the machine (in the form of the railroad) in *fact* penetrated the natural wilderness. Never before did the counterforce disrupt the pastoral middle ground. The American railroad was a symbol become terrifyingly real; and now the middle ground would never again be the same; the railroad would never retreat from the shepherd's quiet life. This irreversible, implacable dislocation moves Channing to respond by setting Walden Spring against the locomotive in his poem and to show how subservient the delights of the garden become to the needs of the machine. More perhaps than any of his contemporaries, Channing felt dislocated by modern industrialism. He had neither the metaphysical support of Emerson nor the imaginative sensuousness of Thoreau to protect himself against an overpowering feeling of helplessness. "Walden Spring" was a heartfelt poem to Channing, one that shows his fears at their deepest and typifies a complex response to the changing face of American life.

The locomotive was an external threat to man's inner life, but Channing knew very well that threats could come from more immediate sources within the spirit. On facing pages in the 1843 *Poems* he published two poems that work through the emotions of loneliness and joy that man finds in nature. These two poems, taken with "Walden Spring," show how thoroughly Channing was aware of the tension between disorder and emotional stability. The first of the two poems, "The Benighted Traveller," is the bleakest poem he ever published:

> He journeys on, slow moving o'er the moor.
> The treacherous dark has razed his homeward path,
> And like a spirit from the heavens sent,
> Dances before him his old kitchen hearth,
> His children round, and antique serving maid.
> The pale stars glimmer through a flickering mist,
> While chill the night-breeze creeps about his heart.
> His unfamiliar step crushes the herb
> That withered long ago, untouched before.
> He stumbles o'er rude stones, and climbs the hill,
> To see the waning moon with pity look
> On marshes spread beneath, and endless glades
> Where never fell his eye until this hour.[24]

The man, moving randomly in the dark, solaced only by his memory, passes through an existence as alien to him as if it were on the moon. In the poem nothing appears capable of ending the isolation and emotional desolation. The images are chosen care-

fully for their cumulative effect: the dark is only teased by the
faint starlight; mist and chill bring physical discomfort matching
the emotional confusion of being lost; the moon finally illuminates
only an unfamiliar, bleak landscape. The poem's theme of despair
conveys all the anguish Channing had tried to escape through his
marriage, friendships, and finally, his writing. It was precisely this
emotional confusion that he was trying to resolve in his pastoral
poems. Just as "Walden Spring" shows how obtrusive the machine
can be, "The Benighted Traveller" shows how man can lose himself. Taken together, the two poems offer examples of how Channing felt thwarted: his culture was rapidly advancing into his
garden of nature; his own emotions were often blighted by despair
and confusion. From within and without, he was menaced by a
paralysis of the spirit.

The alternative to these awful visitations comes in the next
poem, "The River," in which the images of color and movement
strike the senses with pleasure. Where the movement in "The
Benighted Traveller" is halting and futile, the river flows in a
"calm content." The frustrations of loneliness vanish where

> There is an inward voice, that in the stream
> Sends forth its spirit to the listening ear,
> And in a calm content it floweth on,
> Like wisdom, welcome with its own respect.[25]

If no man can escape the miseries of "The Benighted Traveller,"
he can at least plan for daylight on the river; he can deliberately
condition himself to be responsive to nature's beauty. The power
to be renewed, to "smile once more," is the poet's hope in this
poem. As nature so often is in Channing's poetry, it is both reality
and symbol. The river is a concrete representation of the power
nature exerts in his life, but the river is also a physical presence
whose current and lily pads soothe his emotions. The "inward
voice" is the direct, immediate effect nature has on Channing's
psyche. The train's whistle and the rocky landscape at night are
obtrusive realities in the previous poems, but the color and delight of the river are equally real.

Even humility, Channing finds, is possible when he pauses to
examine his relationship with his surroundings. "The Barren
Moors" shows that emotional reserve appropriate to Channing's
view of nature:

On your bare rocks, O barren moors,
On your bare rocks I love to lie,—
They stand like crags upon the shores,
Or clouds upon a placid sky.

Across those spaces desolate,
The fox pursues his lonely way,
Those solitudes can fairly sate
The passage of my loneliest day.

Like desert Islands far at sea
Where not a ship can ever land,
Those dim uncertainties to me,
For something veritable stand.

These three stanzas focus as usual on a landscape, but now roughness, not splendor, dominates the speaker's eye and causes him to
examine the emotions aroused by such a scene. Bare rocks focus
on an empty world with no meaning, and the immediate question
the stanzas raise concerns man's place in such a desolate world.
But the poet sees that even a relatively "empty" nature has a
satisfaction, that they show "something veritable":

A serious place distinct from all
Which busy Life delights to feel,
I stand in this deserted hall,
And thus the wounds of time conceal.

No friend's cold eye, or sad delay,
Shall vex me now where not a sound
Falls on the ear, and every day
Is soft as silence most profound.

No more upon these distant wolds
The agitating world can come,
A single pensive thought upholds
The arches of this dreamy home.

The "busy life" may avoid such desolation, but it also loses sight
of man's ability to know something of himself. The poem implies
that a cheap activity is not inherently good; it is better to be
alone, faced with the rocky landscape than distracted into a futile
life of more activity:

> Within the sky above, one thought
> Replies to you, O barren Moors,
> Between, I stand, a creature taught
> To stand between two silent floors.[26]

The poem's conclusion is a mature recognition that man's best response is neither to flee to companionship nor presumptuously to ask too much from nature. The silence of sky and field is salutary for its composed balance. The speaker is not the universal center of existence, but neither is he a random cipher whose lot is meaningless suffering. If nature could teach such an acceptance of a "chain of being" (so strongly reminiscent of an older idea of man's "station" in life), then it could teach without creating a blinding egotism. Channing's speaker subjects himself to isolation without despair, to questioning without arrogance, and to acceptance without deception.

Therefore, Channing has found in nature a potential world of emotional stability. To respond on this level was to be freed of the torments of self-doubt and intellectual uncertainty. If a poet could call on an imaginative re-creation of man's emotional life, why not turn that creativity toward the best of emotions? From his early poetry to the late, through lyrics and narrative verse, Channing repeatedly shows his readers the beatitude of nature. No matter how pressing the demands of the social and material world, the "ten thousand sights / Of constant nature flow in us, as foams / The bubbling spring; these are the true delights / Wherewith this solemn world the sorrowful requites."[27]

IV *Beauty*

The "solemn world" was for Channing a world drenched in pure beauty unaccompanied by any need of definitions or categories. In his poetry, he assumed a simple syllogism: that which pleases the senses is beautiful; beauty is good; thus, pleasing the senses is good. From the evidence of his own emotions, Channing demanded of poetry an ability to convey beauty through catalogues of pleasing images. In "Wachusett," a poem celebrating New England for its stability, health, and beauty, he writes the following description:

> A yellow tone sweeps southward the horizon,
> The sun to weaving deeper shadows plies on,

More mountains loom, and hills burst up like isles
Shot in the sea by Earth's galvanic piles;
One clear black spot hangs o'er the valley there,
A solitary Hawk balanced on air;
Banks of gray squall-clouds swell below the sun,
The lake turns steel, another sketch begun,
Each instant changes everywhere the scene,
Rapid and perfect turns the Indian screen.[28]

Colors—yellow, black, gray, and gold—movement of light, patterns, clouds, the eye: these are the materials of beauty. If the
human eye is open to what nature provides, the emotions are
soothed, and the speaker feels the benevolence inherent in a perfectly composed landscape. Here is the answer to the railroad
and Lowell's harsh factories; here New England displays a genuine alternative to the vulgarity of industrial growth. His distaste
for the city has led him to find alternatives in a world of color.

The harmony represented by the colors and shapes in such a
scene was for Channing an external sign of an inner harmony.
Nature's beauty exists so that man might have emotional satisfaction. Of a simple country stream, Channing writes:

It went within my inmost heart,
The overhanging Arch to see,
The liquid stream, became a part
Of my internal Harmony.[29]

This correspondence between outer and inner composure was
essential to Channing; for, lacking other forms of stability, he
turned to nature. Sympathies, Channing called them, these emotional bonds between men and nature's objects: "To mark the Day
sink calmly down, / While burning hills to shadow fade, / How
deep are Nature's sympathies / How soon her mute demands
obeyed!"[30] The responsive, self-reliant man could share these
sympathies. Here in a simple openness, Channing found his humanity affirmed. Through such verse—the kind Emerson repeatedly encouraged him to write—he tenaciously worked toward
a style of living that affirms, not denies, man's possibilities. His
was a life that had human responses, not the abstractions of materialism.

A poem that developed from Channing's many visits to Thoreau's hut at Walden makes more precise the satisfactions of nature's benevolent beauty. Without unseemly affectation, the opening describes the pond's attractiveness:

> It is not far beyond the Village church,
> After we pass the wood that skirts the road,
> A Lake,—the blue-eyed Walden, that doth smile
> Most tenderly upon its neighbor pines,
> And they as if to recompense this love,
> In double beauty spread their branches forth.
> This Lake had tranquil loveliness and breadth,
> And of late years has added to its charms,
> For one attracted to its pleasant edge,
> Has built himself a little Hermitage,
> Where with much piety he passes life.

Channing finds added delight in nature's unexpected plenty. An already graceful scene is duplicated in the water's reflection by extending the graceful line of trees downward as well as up. As if naturally allied to this increased beauty, Thoreau has now made his life a part of the landscape. Virtue—an important form of beauty in Emerson's definition—has now enhanced the visual attractiveness of the pond. This union of a natural setting and a moral life is captured in Channing's next image:

> More fitting place I cannot fancy now,
> For such a man to let the line run off
> The mortal reel, such patience hath the lake,
> Such gratitude and cheer is in the Pines.

Thoreau knew well the necessity of finding an environment to match his inner exploration. Channing's image fits not only an extended description but a quality of Thoreau's experience that Channing recognized well. In Thoreau, he had found a virtue of large proportions; in Walden's beauty he found a landscape to match:

> But more than either lake or forest's depths,
> This man has in himself; a tranquil man,
> With sunny sides where well the fruit is ripe,
> Good front, and resolute bearing to this life,

And some serener virtues, which control
This rich exterior prudence, virtues high,
That in the principles of Things are set,
Great by their nature and consigned to him,
Who, like a faithful Merchant, does account
To God for what he spends, and in what way.

The self-knowledge and composure in Thoreau is a natural extension of the poem's opening description of Walden Pond. Here was a man capable of settling his accounts with God each day. The husbandry of such living had escaped the paltry waste common to other men because this life increased in beauty just as the pond had increased by its reflection. Here, needing neither artifice of abstraction nor material accumulation, was a life as beautiful as the pond. Nothing external is needed because each complements the other in the same way that the reflection has complemented the woods. The poem's conclusion takes the appropriate tone:

Thrice happy art thou, Walden! in thyself,
Such purity is in thy limpid springs;
In those green shores which do reflect in thee,
And in this man who dwells upon thy edge,
A holy man within a Hermitage.
May all good showers fall gently into thee,
May thy surrounding forests long be spared,
And may the Dweller on thy tranquil shores,
There lead a life of deep tranquillity
Pure as thy Waters, handsome as thy Shores
And with those virtues which are like the Stars.[31]

The threefold beauty is a triple blessing to Channing. The satisfaction of tranquility as naturally evolves from such a life as the beauty of the pond evolves from its visual composition. The final union of pond and man with the stars makes the final development of beauty. From a triple beauty the speaker finds a quadruple as the scene is merged with the beauty of the stars. From landscape to transcendent beauty, Channing's poem moves carefully across the visual, emotional, and spiritual spectrum.

Very typically in this poem Channing uses his "memory" as the imaginative vehicle. Repeatedly his world of "dreams," memories, and other imaginative processes became the most satisfactory source of images to combine the external, sensory reality of nature with his inner, emotional life. Beauty, he saw, had its reality in the life of the beholder; and the subjective life was all that counted. With good reason, he scorned Thoreau's careful note-taking and thorough journal keeping. His well-known outburst to Thoreau—"*I* am universal"—sounds affected out of context, but in the light of his poetry, Channing's attitude is less pompous. He had an "inward mirror" he said, that reflected beauty and made it meaningful. "Dreams! I revere them," Channing says triumphantly in "To the Reader," the poem introducing *Conversations in Rome:*

>   may we not dispel
> The shadowy visions that within us dwell!
> Bright shapes and fiery forms, be those our care,
> And a gay landscape float around them fair,
> Have solid gold for ceiling of their earth,
> And in the dust a planetary worth!
> Let the Soul journey in the land of dream,
> And never may the day, with flattering beam,
> Look in and light that land; let us see Rome,
> As she stands firm within the Fancy's home.

Beauty and nature have made a rich internal world for Channing. The inner "Rome" of the dream, the fancy, counts more for him than the city of marble and brick. Failing, he thought, to find an external world free of the industrial "counterforce," he would create for himself an idyllic inner life. "The land of dream" was better than Concord; the purely subjective life was finally the life of the poet:

> For never on such shapes the sun shall set
> As rise within thee; all things else forget,—
> Thy friend, thy work, whatever thou dost know,—
> Let all decease, and keep thy faith below,
> In the austerer cities of thy soul,
> Founded where winds and rains have no control;

The dream world was impervious to time—no decay worked on the fancy. Those "austere" cities of man's inner life are truly more

substantial than the physical world. His friends had thought
Channing foolish to leave Rome after only sixteen days, but he
had confirmed what he already knew: "The sands of Europe
gleam on Salem's shore."[32]

Here Channing has made his own emotions, memories, and
dreams Marx's "middle ground." He would later in his career return to New England as the place where the pastoral vision could
in fact be realized, but the American pastoral becomes for him in
his shorter poems a private world perfectly protected against
time, the railroad, and personal frustrations. He responded to the
challenges of his time by creating a radical subjectivism. Without
an ultimate test of reality, such as that open to Emerson or Thoreau, Channing was the most lonely Transcendentalist. Like Hawthorne, he had his own dungeon of the heart, but poetry was his
key to a larger world, a more responsive self. That ability to make
beauty the source of psychic peace gave him the life he needed.
Restless as he was with industrial New England, convinced as he
became that only poetry was a possible alternative, Channing
trusted his own responses to nature's beauty.

V *Self-Reliance*

At no point does Channing come closer to Emerson and
Thoreau than in his desire to create a unique *self* capable of having ever more intense experiences. An ode honoring Emerson in
1857 expresses the importance of self-knowledge to Channing:

> In other lands they might have worshipped him;
> Nations had stood and blocked their chariot wheels
> At his approach—towns stooped beneath his foot!
> But here, in our vast wilderness, he walks
> Alone—if 't is to be alone when stars
> And breath of summer mountain airs and morn
> And the wild music of the untempered sea
> Consort with human genius.[33]

Here is power expressed in the magnetism of self-reliance. Channing realizes that only he who has command of his own powers
can make an impression of the world around him. Mountains,
stars, and the sea are fitting companions for the true individualists;
for only such men have tapped the power of nature.

Were a man to cultivate his fancy, his imaginative responsive-

ness, Channing thought, he might begin to come near that source
of strength, nature. Reflecting on some paintings given him, he
says:

> Ah glorious fancy, who with shaping skill
> Hast visited us here, else how obscure,
> And with thy splendid charms and graceful mien
> Re-clothed the sere and tearful, drooping world,[34]

The self-possession that comes through a "shaping skill" makes
possible knowledge and emotional peace, two more of life's neces-
sities. Because he can respond, man can transform the potential
in his life into active experience that "we had wished to live." An
attention to "fancy," Channing insists, asserts genuine possibilities
of joy, knowledge, and renewal. In a dramatic fragment published
in *The Dial*, he says:

> Whoever knew not living
> Some of his inner self; who had no consciousness
> Of all his purposes, his doings,—will?
> Why this we call the mind, what is it, save
> A knowledge of ourselves?[35]

Here again the control man can exert waits only his will, only his
self-possession. The optimistic tone conveys Channing's unshakable belief that a truly unique self could be created and that
power could be exerted on nature once a man had found the
courage of self-reliance.

One of his most imaginative poems brings into focus the combination of nature and will that Channing had found necessary
in his own life. "The Lonely Road," a poem from the 1846 volume,
opens with a simple but evocative landscape:

> No track had worn the lone deserted road,
> Save where the Fox had leapt from wall to wall;
> There were the swelling, glittering piles of snow,
> Up even with the walls, and save the Crow
> Who lately had been pecking Barberries,
> No other signs of life beyond ourselves.

The desolation in this scene prepares the reader for that of the
ruined farm which next appears, and Channing takes care to

evolve human meanings from the barrenness of the landscape.
The world of the fox and crow have specific analogues in a more
human world. The tone remains consistent as the images shift to
man's perspective:

> We strayed along, beneath our feet the lane
> Creaked at each pace, and soon we stood content
> Where the old cellar of the house had been,
> Out of which now a fruit-tree wags its top.
> Some scraggy orchards hem the landscape round,
> A forest of sad Apple-trees unpruned,
> And then a newer orchard pet of him,
> Who in his dotage kept this lonely place.
> In this wild scene, and shut-in Orchard dell,
> Men like ourselves, once dwelt by roaring fires,
> Loved this still spot, nor had a further wish.
> A little wall half falling bounds a square
> Where choicer fruit-trees showed the Garden's pride,
> Now crimsoned by the Sumach, whose red cones
> Displace the colors of the cultured growth.

The fruit trees—the scene's visual center—exude a decay made
more exact through the contrasting color of sumach and apples.
The scene, once dominated by the colorful fruit, is now "gone
wild." Once a source of food, the orchards have lost their cultiva-
tion and surrender to rankness.

The desolation moves the speaker to remember scenes of happier days that contrast with his depression:

> I know not how it is, that in these scenes
> There is a desolation so complete,
> It tarries with me after I have passed,
> And the dense growth of woodland, or a sight
> Of distant Cottages or landscapes wide,
> Cannot obscure the dreary, cheerless thought.
> But why should I remember those once there,
> And think of childish voices, or that kind
> Caressing hands of tender parents gone,
> Have twined themselves in that soft golden hair,
> All fled, and silent as an unlit Cave.
> Why should I stand and muse upon their lives,
> Who for me truly never had more life,

> Than in the glancing mind's eye; or in Fancy
> Wear this irrespective form, thus fleeting.

Time seems inescapable to a man alive to such desolation. The memories merely reënforce the isolation he is experiencing: he no more felt the presence of the farm's residents then than he can now. Each visual image—tree, sumach, fence, and garden—depresses him. Only his "Fancy," his imaginative faculty, can transform the depressed emotions into a human triumph:

> I people the void scene with Fancy's eye,
> Her children do not live too long for me,
> They vibrate in the house whose walls I rear,
> The mansion as themselves, the fugitives
> Of my Intent in this soft Winter day.
> Nor will I scatter these faint images,
> Idle as shadows that the tall reeds cast
> Over the silent ice, beneath the moon,
> For in these lonely haunts where Fancy dwells,
> And evermore creating weaves a veil
> In which all this that we call life abides,
> There must be deep retirement from the day,
> And in these shadowy vistas we shall meet,
> Sometime the very Phantom of ourselves.—
> A long Farewell, thou dim and silent spot,
> Where serious Winter sleeps, or the soft hour,
> Of some half dreamy Autumn afternoon;
> And may no idle feet tread thy domain,
> But only men to Contemplation vowed,
> Still as ourselves, creators of the Past.[36]

The speaker finds a quiet release from sorrow and despondency through his own power of rejuvenation. The strength of "Fancy's eye" is the strength of self-possession—the strength of a man who can respond to nature through his imagination. Protected against the emotional paralysis that the scene invites, he refuses to grovel before time's inevitable decay because he has an interior life. The colors and forms in nature combine with imagination to "weave a veil" of heightened understanding. Sensitivity, creation, and tranquility merge in the speaker's responses. Channing has found the "Phantom" self in his retirement from life's distracting commerce. To be a "creator of the Past" is to be alive to imagination.

"The Lonely Road" shows how far Channing had taken Emerson's credo of self-reliance, for the poem contains an exploration of living outside society. The poem suggests that those moments of heightened life occur in isolation, that only a self-communion made possible by the colors and shapes in nature comes finally to be satisfying. This ideal of selfhood raises Channing to visions of ecstasy in "The Sibyl to Her Lover" in the 1843 *Poems*. The poem's fifteen stanzas make an intense plea for the sort of self-conscious, self-creating life that Channing found most satisfying. Midway through the poem, the sibyl warns of the dangers of relaxation:

> Wait but the hour,—thy course is run;
> Life's carpentry will build no more;
> Thou shalt sit silenced in the dun,
> Perpetual tempests' sluggish roar;
> Those velvet tresses soft and free,
> Slimed and disfigured then shall be.

The image of befouled beauty is Channing's warning to cautious men. With Emerson and Whitman, he adds his voice to the plea for a standard of life that cuts through our cloying routine and that holds up the possibility of a life more open to the imagination. The next stanza shifts the metaphor from restriction to freedom:

> Bide not thy time, heed not thy fate,
> Believe no truth, respect no law,
> Fling to the winds foul custom's state,
> And play with every antique saw;
> For in thee hides a matchless light,
> That splendors all the dreaming night.

Channing's familiar "dreaming night" invokes again his world of the imagination (here contrasted to the routine of "custom"). The inner "light" lies in all men; the poet calls for the reliance on self that frees men to explore new regions of their being.

The image of a boat then dominates the poem's final stanzas:

> Thy bark shall be a precious stone,
> In whose red veins deep magic hides;
> Thy ecstasies be known to none,
> Except those vast perpetual tides

> Which circulate the world's wide round,
> But whisper not the slightest sound.[37]

He often writes of sailing, of release, and joy; and his "barks" are imaginative journeys into exuberance. Here the sensory delight of color, the connotation of immense value, and the freedom of the boat bring together the emotional stimulations Channing keeps at the center of verse. The self-reliant man is the true "sailor" who sails a sea in quest of a triumph over artificial limitations. Once having made this article of faith in man's potential "self," Channing can open his next poem, "A Poet's Hope," with a triumphant optimism:

> Flying,—flying beyond all lower regions,
> Beyond the light called day, and night's repose,
> Where the untrammelled soul, on her wind-pinions
> Fearlessly sweeping, defies my earthly woes;—
> There,—there, upon that infinitest sea,
> Lady, thy hope,—so fair a hope, summons me.

The two poems are a unit: the sibyl speaks of possibility, and the poet answers with a responsiveness that underlies Channing's ideas about man's relationship to nature. Finally, having worked through these emotions, he can close "A Poet's Hope" with his well-known line: "If my bark sinks, 't is to another sea,"[38] which now sounds more like Channing's subjectivism than a Transcendental credo. The fully realized self-reliant man has a depth, a multiplicity of "seas," that he himself has created. The images of sea and boats are as consistent as those of dreams and visions as Channing's poetic devices for answering the apostles of progress. He was a poet firmly convinced that his art was salvation, that only the energy of imagination was sufficient to answer those men who were only too glad to see that "things" are in the saddle.

After the machine came to the garden in the 1840's, the old ideal of a pastoral haven had to be remade; therefore, Channing made the garden in his own soul, used the external beauty of nature as his source, and lived most fully through his poetry. Self-reliance, beauty, and nature merged in his subjective life of the emotions as his response to the encroachment of industrial power. What finally freed him was the realization that his life grew only insofar as he could "trust thyself" and live according to that trust.

Channing recognized this fact early in his life; and, despite the paradoxes we have seen, he accepted the challenge. "I will not sing for gain, nor yet for fame," he said; for he had found his reward within himself.[39]

VI *Transcendentalism*

Ellery Channing has always been identified as one of the lesser, more spectacularly errant American Transcendentalists. A close friend to the major figures of the period, an advocate of nature's delight, self-reliance, and withdrawal from all social questions, he obviously has a place in that very diverse group; but that place is not at all easily defined. To lump him in with the "minor Transcendentalists" or to dismiss him as an odd poet of uncertain temperament would be to lose sight, first, of what he accomplished and, second, of what American Transcendentalism emphasized. Unlike Emerson and Thoreau, who struggled to develop consistent and substantial intellectual points of view, Channing had neither the inclination nor the patience to define his position with such rigor. Nor did he share the same faith that informed the best work of his friends, for, when contrasted to them, Channing was a "casual" Transcendentalist.

The central principle in Transcendentalism is an intuition of the reality of a divine immanence. From this assumption, it follows that man partakes of divinity, that God is *in* man. This union is anterior to and necessary for the Transcendentalist's concern with self-reliance (the divine self-sufficiency of the individual), nature (the externalization of divinity), and social reform (the bringing of society into conformity with, in Emerson's words, the "divine idea"). Channing simply lacked this religious conviction: neither his poetry nor his informal manuscripts express a central concern for deity. He acknowledges a conventional "belief" in God, but this faith was neither a motivation for his poetry nor a principle guiding his personal life. In an unpublished poem, he explicitly rejects Transcendentalism as a label: "It makes me laugh / When I am called, / By thy long name, / And in thy church installed." He goes on to sympathize with Transcendentalism (it is, after all, preferable to a devastating materialism), but he knew enough about himself to know that, at this point, he was quite different from many of his contemporaries:

> Transcendentalist I am,
> Or thus the stupid say
> Who garnish this dark universe,
> With their refulgent day,
> And though this word
> Means little to my ear,
> Tis better than some strains I've heard,
> Which I did know & fear.[40]

Most often Channing retreats to a conventional theism which is little different in conception from the Unitarian "God"—a personal but hazily defined center of the universe.

With his distaste for intellectual rigor, Channing never matched the depth of Emerson or Alcott: Swedenborg, for instance, made no impression on him. Unlike his closest friends—Thoreau, Margaret Fuller, and Emerson—Channing apparently never had moments of ecstatic revelation. The mystical experiences which catapulted his friends beyond phenomena into an immediate, undeniable experience of Transcendental unity never came to him. More in response to these friends than to any experience of his own came his occasional tributes to an ideal reality. He could say in "Una" that "We are centered deeper far / Than the eye of any star";[41] but the poems of his lifetime fail to support the assertion as a motivating belief in Channing. Too interested in the immediate effect nature had on the emotions to probe metaphysics, his curiosity stopped with phenomena; the human, not the divine, reality challenged him to write. He rubbed his mind against Emerson and Thoreau, but he came away with a renewed interest in nature, not in the most fundamental Transcendental assumption.

VIII   A Poet's Hope

Lacking this religious motivation, what caused Channing to write for over sixty years? What assumptions lie behind this profusion of poems? The answers to these questions begin with his life-long belief that most men waste their lives. Like Emerson, whose essays are as ethical as they are metaphysical, Channing announces in his poetry a revulsion against shabby living, against material and emotional complacency. He, with his friends, wanted to be judged by the *quality* of his experiences. Were the emotions heightened? Did the sympathy, generosity, and benevolence latent in a man ever have the chance for development? He acknowledged a "crass casuality" in his poems: creativity might be suspended; the emotions depressed; death stalks all men. Still, other facts, other experiences are compensatory; for other possibilities of enjoyment are to be had if man will only renounce his lust for goods and his weak will.

Nature—the recognition of beauty and calm, the untapped stock of emotional satisfaction—takes the center of Channing's imagination. He glorifies the common experience, the trivial action so long as it has nature's setting for validity. As much as any of his contemporaries, he tried to dramatize the inherent value of the most ordinary details. Flower, color, creek, vine—each reveals restorative potential. This body of poetry is grounded in the native American pastoral ideal: work is sanctified by contact with the soil; the senses, undisturbed by urban or social intrusions, make a standard of value. Simple pleasure is equated with virtue.

Above all, stability and emotional repose are essential to such poetry. Without the repeated establishment of quietude as a value of incalculable proportion, the poetry would not escape a mean dilettantism. For Channing, though, the recovery of an emotional center was fundamental to a man's life. His own uncertainties naturally brought him to this kind of poetry, but the poems are more than a working out of his own tensions. The poet becomes a symbolic man who summons the courage to dream, to oppose the shabby loss of vitality in life, and to trust his own emotions. That subjective standard of beauty and ecstasy that permeates his poetry assumes a self-trust and a faith in a human nobility.

To Channing, the ideal of a life well lived was inseparable from poetry; for to write was to live truly because the poet has a duty to announce his optimism. The hours with Thoreau in Canada, or on Cape Cod, were hours that made a poet. Only from such experiences could poetry come; only from poetry could men be shown healthy alternatives to their emotional disquietudes. Writing and living thus blend for Channing; living the life of a poet takes on specific characteristics: not only writing, but talking, observing, and dreaming. Each activity was a part of a whole; each new poem an invitation to live more fully.

CHAPTER *5*

New England and the Pastoral Ideal

AS Channing grew older, new directions of form and thought emerged from his poetry. In the three decades from 1858 to 1886 he published four book-length narrative poems that continue the familiar themes he had been pursuing since his youth, but they gradually move outward from the highly subjective world of the "dream" that marks his shorter verse into a more socially conscious attitude. The first two books of poems, *Near Home* (1858) and *The Wanderer* (1871), are Channing's contributions to a fully pastoral literature tied closely to New England as a region. In them, we see him coming away from the "simple pastoral" that Marx describes into a more complex pastoralism that recognized the irony of counterforce and the ambiguity of man's responses to nature. In the final two poems, *Eliot* (1885) and *John Brown and the Heroes of Harper's Ferry* (1886), all we can see is the long decline of Transcendentalism's best qualities; for the poems of Channing's old age are his least effective ones.

I Near Home

True to Channing's consistent hatred of city life, he contrasts in *Near Home* the New England countryside with the city where "slow corruption breathes, / Infests the air, and with its sallow host / Spawns ragged children for as ragged sire."[1] The old sense of waste and loss still weighs heavily on the poet; and, as throughout his work, he seems almost desperate in beholding how vainly men live in the cities. His dissatisfaction with Boston, the rural idealism of his prose, and the subjective satisfaction of the lyric poems are all united in his fear of a corrupted life.

A pair of contrasting images in *Near Home* return Channing to the healing powers of nature:

> Not on the high road, not in dusty cars
> Loud-thundering o'er their iron vertebrae,
> Where in close boxes sweltering with the speed
> Nod in newspaper dreams the broadcloth world;—
> Nor with capricious haste of foaming steeds,
> Essay thou, rather along the river's smooth
> Untenanted domain gliding in peace,
> Steal with soft fancies in a silent bark.[2]

The train and boat are naturally opposed images for Channing. The train captures the noise, heat, dust, and lack of comfort in man's artificial style of living; the boat (as in the earlier poems) is the object of freedom, quiet, and pleasure. The contrast in *Near Home* between nature and man's created world is simple and un- qualified: the artificial is balanced by the natural, the ugly by the beautiful, and the powerful by the delightful. The train as an image of contrast possesses extensive negative connotations; but, if we remember the disruptive locomotive of "Walden Spring," we see that this image of the railroad is less challenging: where the first was the instrument of a shattering force, the train image in *Near Home* focuses on the uninterrupted pleasure nature still offers man.

   Nature gains a complexity in *Near Home* in Channing's new insistence on a resurrection in nature:

> This resurrection of the buried earth,
> This weaving of new garments in an hour
> For our else naked orb, her fairest moment
> In the whole long day, must fail the weariest hand.
> Yet what these few faint touches may convey,
> Be that conveyed.[3]

This image of spring is conventional, but Channing was finding in 1858 new powers of personality in his approach to nature. Only two years after Ellen's death, he was recovering from the dark days of the early 1850's when his life was most bleak, his emo- tions most uncertain. Newness and fresh sources of personal power were much in his mind and emotions as he writes:

> Perpetual newness and the health in things.
> This, is the startling theme, the lovely birth

Each morn of a new day, so wholly new,
So absolutely penetrated by itself,
The fresh, the fair, the ever-living grace, . . .[4]

In these lines Channing reveals his sympathy with nature's moods. Recovering from a long night of frustration, pain, and loneliness, he responds fully to nature's renewal and health. The shift in this poem is slight but significant: earlier poems had focused on the fullness of experience and the joy of sensory stimulation, but now in *Near Home* the poet marvels at the renewal of life itself. Very much in the background of this poem is a pronounced fear that the darkness of death has been very close to the speaker. The poem opens with an image of relief: "Still burns at Heaven's gate thy golden torch, / All-conquering Sun, and in thy flame at morn / The wearied nations rise."[5] The otherwise conventional hymn to nature is made more complex by a latent fear of death and blight.

Coming from this more complex attitude was a greater sense in Channing of the effect New England was having on him and of the possibility that the region could be raised to symbolic heights. His sense of "place" and his need for a "home" were merging in this poem:

Here thou canst repose
And dream away the pains of ardent life,
Forego ambition and the world's applause,
Stretching along the bank, fanned by the wind
That even in summer heats, from the cool surface
Quaffs a breath of life, forget thy madness,
Thy contriving wit, that made thee stoop
To things beneath thyself.[6]

New England was just the place of repose: its physical beauty was unquestionable; its traditions of independence encouraged each man to find his own style of living. It was a place where man could indeed "Clasp palm to nature's palm."[7]

To focus on the power a man gains when he finds himself at home in his land, Channing opens his poem with a verse dedication to Thoreau, his "ideal man," as we have seen in Chapter 3. Because Thoreau insisted on living a life of virtue, because he was a "pastoral man" living close to the land, Channing invokes his aid. He recognizes a power in Thoreau to "compel," to chal-

lenge lesser men to new heights of creation. The friendship so
necessary to both Thoreau and Channing that is to occupy us in
the next chapter is in this poem a symbolic relationship between
a man of psychic wholeness and the poem's narrator who is looking for his "home."

Faith in a pastoral idyll was strong in New England. Emerson
and Thoreau had a faith more complex than Channing's, but
others—Margaret Fuller, Alcott, and many obscure men of good
will—longed for that escape from the cares of the city that country life promised. Such a response is, in Marx's words, "widely
diffused in our culture, insinuating itself into many kinds of behavior."[8] Not surprisingly, Channing responds to this feeling and
tries to make it a literal part of his life. His insecurity and loneliness naturally turned him to nature as relief and gratification for
those emotions of love and dignity that he too seldom found
among men. But Channing is not content merely to respond: he
spent a lifetime trying to make the simple ideal take form in more
complex symbolic, verbal forms. He has both the openness of the
sentimental pastoral ideal and the sophistication of a poet. For
this reason, he looked carefully for the symbols to capture the
complexity as well as the openness of America's relationship to
nature.

New England—the locale, the "home"—becomes in *Near Home*
his focus for the conviction that man's life could be renovated:

> Here, in these shades, these deep seclusions hid
> Beneath the whisp'ring leaves and o'er our moors
> A ragged independence lives at ease,
> Wearing those good adornments of the race,
> Such as pure air, warm suns, and builds the Hero
> Urban pens describe.[9]

That "ragged independence" was the source for a true brotherhood (Channing, Thoreau, and Alcott for instance, *were* men of
slim means whose bare subsistence was one source of their love
for each other). Moreover, New England provided just the image
to catch the contrast between a false wealth of things and a true
wealth of spirit:

> I had rather be,
> The meanest worm that haunts our berry-fields,
> Than wear the purple on those distant thrones,

And love far more the breath of Liberty
Across our poor, uncultured, sandy soils,
Than all the crumbling empires in their shrouds.[10]

Symbolically, ideally, New England is the superior "home" for
men who value their souls. Looking for a focus for his values, his
fears, and his optimism, Channing turned in this first long narrative poem to his region for his symbol. He is responding to a
deeply felt need to find a place for himself, to find an external
symbol for his need of a true identity. Here, in a world where
one could enjoy the "wealth of Penury,"[11] he had moved beyond
the earlier poems that celebrated only a personal, sensual stimulation.

II   The Wanderer

When Channing again took up the theme of "place" in a narrative poem, he completed his emotional journey from the less
complex subjectivity of his earlier work to a more complex recog-
nation of the tensions between man's love of nature and the forces
working against the fulfillment of that pastoral idealism. *The
Wanderer* is organized in seven parts that allow the narrator to
survey New England's physical and historical realities and see
more fully how this particular "home" frees the imagination.
While the poem has close kinship with the rest of Channing's
work, it takes him into new areas of awareness. He says of the
poet: "I think whate'er he found he loved; kneeling / As some
dread worshipper before the shrine, / Wholly desirous to be one
with God."[12] But this adoration is now threatened by more intense, complex fears of death, of the counterforce of technology,
and of the geological immensity of the landscape.

In a passage of the sort Marx describes as almost archetypical
in its frequent appearance in American writing, Channing evokes
his full awareness of satisfying but awesome qualities in nature:

I hurry forward where the leafless trees
Are wrapped in silence, as the red cold light
Of January's sunset touches each
As with a fire of icicles,—how calm!
Oh! transient gleams yon hurrying noisy train,
Its yellow carriages rumbling with might
Of volleyed thunder on the iron rail

Pieced by the humble toil of Erin's hand,
Wood and lake the whistle shrill awakening.
Transient,—contrast with the unthinking cold,
The ruddy glare of sunset in the west,
And the first flicker of the icy stars,
While the pale freezing moon calmly assists
To point their rays more sharp,—transient and stern![13]

Initially, the oxymoron "fire of icicles" and the "red" but "cold" light establishes the emotional tension inherent in the scene. The colors and gleaming surface are delightful, but the natural qualification of the chill prepares the scene for the train's intrusion. Here nature, so long the symbol and presence of emotional satisfaction in Channing's life, has been pierced by the counterforce of technology. The overtone of time's passing is an additional qualification the locomotive suggests. The complex balance in the poem of sensory delight and disruptive foreboding is brought to a close with the images of cold light from the moon and stars. The landscape is delightful but frozen; the train is both a technological fact and a symbol of time's passing. This ironic suspension of images has brought Channing to his most complex reaction to the American pastoral ideal. The locomotive is the industrial counterforce challenging the simple pleasure of the landscape. Delight and fear come together; the poet's response catches the ambiguous situation. Here is a clear example of how Channing has made the transition from the simple, naïve pastoral ideal to the complex pastoral work of art. Even at a time when the Romantic spirit of Concord had waned, when Transcendental enthusiasm had given way to the growth of Naturalism, Channing was continuing his imaginative search for a "home."

    The Wanderer introduces a second form of an ironic counterforce when the poet finds in the seashore a reminder of nature's ageless creativity combined with an awesome power:

> Oh! what a day, and night of days, swept by,
> As, slowly o'er the gray unmoving hills,
> In endless march deployed the polar host!
> Oh! what an hour when that sea-tossing mass
> Began to cut the coast-lines, and map out
> The rays of a few continents, and drop
> Their bowlders [sic] in the path![14]

The ice cap that remade the shore line is the essence of power to Channing, for here he contemplates a primitive wildness beyond the "middle ground" of his pastoral poems. Nature, he abruptly sees, retains for herself a margin of mystery whose impact on the emotions is ambiguous at best; for the power to make is equally a power to destroy.

These images of time (the railroad) and of space (geological immensity) have revealed Channing's more complex reactions to nature. The ambiguity (quite an unfamiliar reaction in his earlier poems) is a direct challenge to his faith in the senses and in a natural simplicity—and to his assumption that man makes for himself an unqualified triumph by living in nature. In this poem, the wanderer may well be lost in an overwhelming natural world.

To resolve this emotional ambiguity, Channing turns to myth and history where other men have faced and understood this relationship to nature. He invokes the spirit of the sea as his preparation: "Dreaming the sea the elder, I must search / In her for tidings of the olden days,— / Oldest and newest."[15] The sea speaks of Babylon, of Rome, and of England, showing the poet that, through the development of civilization, man has sought his freedom: the New World is the apex of an evolutionary quest. If both time and space dwarf man, they work through history and geology finally to man's benefit. Channing has found his protection against an ambiguous fear of time and technology: no matter how destructive the power to change, the power to re-create ever keeps a balance. Like the theme of renewal in *Near Home,* the theme of cosmic balance in *The Wanderer* allows him to deal with a complex reaction to his fear of corruption and to his faith in creativity. The pastoral theme in the poem encompasses both past and present, both the middle ground and the wildness of nature, both the counterforce of technology and the sensory delight of beauty. Nature is grand and awesome, but Channing has kept his poem within a human perspective.

He uses this renewed faith in New England to examine the corruption he saw undercutting his "home." He faces the growing inequality of wealth created by the industrialization of the society when he says:

> Can we sink
> The dark and dangerous classes in the mire,
> Safely obliterate? and at our ease

> Napping behind the curtains, and delight
> With spendthrift opulence of ill-got wealth,
> And sideboard blazed with plate, omit the claim
> Of human misery, fainting at the door?[16]

While this passage is similar to the other Channing attacks on materialism, he is now aware of the disparity between democratic faith and social reality. Were the gap between the ideal of industrial dignity and actual poverty to grow wider, he thought, America's future would be endangered.

The same greed that oppresses the poor Irish corrodes the possibility of creating an American "Imagination." Using the contrast of a mythic splendor of the sea with the New England fishery, Channing writes:

> Idalian Venus, on her pink conch-shell,
> Smoothing the lovely wave, and throwing smiles
> Over the laughing billows. But to-day
> To the depths descend the gods of ocean,
> When mackerel fishers ride the hollow main,
> And in the room of Phosphor, worship gold.[17]

Man has always found the sea an imaginative power, and its myths and legends have meant much to him. But, to Channing, America is losing touch with this poetic imagination; when cash supersedes myth, culture is impoverished.

That connection between the art of poetry and the world of myth and history intrigued Channing:

> Surest of all the facts of mortal life
> Men symbolize the meaning of the thoughts;
> The Indian on his skin painting his bears,
> And strange Peruvian on his quipo knots
> Writing his stanza, down to Europe's pride,
> Even to demonic Goethe, feats in words;[18]

The ability to use symbols makes man aware of himself, and the duty of the poem comes to be the life's salvation for the wanderer. Channing was obviously justifying his life of writing, but he was also expressing a faith in America as a community willing to listen to its modern mythmakers. The world of nature that New Eng-

land presents to the rest of the nation is material enough for the
imaginative powers to act on:

> Rich with Valhalla's and metheglin's fume.
> But we might launch our gods, as they sang theirs,
> Even as our clime and seasons native spring,
> So now from us upsprings the myth to-day,
> Or shall ere morning gild yon russet field?
> Each holds his office, each his native skill,
> By self in one part poised, by fate as much:
> The rose can never bloom the lily's white,
> Nor a still day usurp the whirlwind's roar.[19]

The wanderer has now come to New England; the ambiguities of
time and space find their emotional and intellectual release
through the evocation of a historical mythic past and of a poetic
future. New England is now a mythic land: the representative
"home" for men who would truly live. Channing has moved his
own world of satisfaction outward until he sees his "home" as the
place where all men might be at one with nature, escape the city,
and know a freedom from the ambiguities of time.

   The Wanderer is a fitting climax to Channing's career, for it
most fully recognizes the values inherent in the American pastoral
ideal while it responds to the ironic counterforces working against
the fulfillment of that dream. Through the letters of the young
poet and artist, Channing had voiced the discontentment his
generation had felt with the quality of American life. Then, in
the lyric poems and *Conversations in Rome,* he had explored his
private satisfaction with dreams and sensory stimulation. Finally,
at the threshold of old age he came in *The Wanderer* and in
Thoreau: The Poet-Naturalist to a full statement of his hopes and
fears that he could show in both poem and biography how a really
full life could be lived.

   To give the poem a better focus, Channing creates idealized
portraits of his friends; and Thoreau, Emerson, and Margaret
Fuller emerge in an ideal form as symbolic inhabitants of the
land. Like similar idealized scenes in *Near Home,* these portraits
lack the particularity and accuracy of realistic description, but
they show how Channing responded to his friends. Margaret
Fuller is "Composedly thoughtful, genial, yet reserved, / Pure as
the wells that dot the ravine's bed, / And lofty as the stars that

pierce her skies."[20] Though she had been a faithful sister-in-law, she was hardly such a queen as he describes. Emerson was the "sage of his days, patient and proudly true, / Whose word was worth the world, whose heart was pure."[21] These examples of what friendship meant to Channing prepare us for an understanding of the complex relationships between the Concord writers: he shared with them a need for a unique "home" and for friendships that spurred the imagination. His tribute to Thoreau reflects how important in this context friendship was:

> In a self-comfortable pride resolved
> To equalize things mundane. Much he sought
> The limit of the exact. He testified
> By painful art how much his world produced,
> Precisely how he stood with every fact
> Wherein co-adjutor with Nature's truth; . . .[22]

Friendship was a reality, finally, to satisfy Channing's need to feel at home. *The Wanderer* gathers together this relationship between the pastoral life, the counterforce of time and space, and friendship. Here is the "home" for Channing's symbolic wanderer. He had been on a "journey" since 1834 when he left Harvard: his trip West, his marriage, career, and friendships all added to the creation of New England's "wanderer." From subjective delight in the senses, Channing has moved to a dramatization of New England as the representative land for representative men. His delight in personal stimulation has been raised now to the possibility of all America's finding an identity, of seeing how whole men can become. The pastoral ideal comes to its most mature form in this poem as Channing writes of the challenge to our simple faith in renewal and of the possible life which recognizes that challenge.

III Eliot

By 1873, Channing's effective career had ended. With the publication in 1871 of *The Wanderer* and in 1873 of *Thoreau: The Poet-Naturalist*, he had completed his journey from a Romantic subjectivity to a shared community. If *Near Home* and *The Wanderer* are not fully satisfactory poems to modern readers, they show clearly how the impulses of Transcendentalism with its self-reliance, its appeal to dignity, and its emotional stimulation could be raised to a broad context. Those faiths of the 1840's had a place in 1870 and 1880, but the creative force behind them had faded. The American intellectual life had moved on under the influence of Charles Darwin, Auguste Comte, and Herbert Spencer. Prose had become the most creative form of imaginative expression. Without the force of Emerson or Thoreau or the radical simplicity of Bronson Alcott, the Transcendentalists had nothing out of which to work. Channing, who kept the faith, wrote more poetry about nature and self-reliance, but he did so in a vacuum. Before the Civil War, he had commanded respect as a figure within a larger creative world. On his own in the strange light of the Gilded Age, he was only a lonely old man.

His next book, *Eliot* (1885), shows the deflation of his world. A long narrative poem, *Eliot* is a diary of a frontier hermit dying of remorse over a duel in which he has killed a rival. The poem is full of Gothic gimcracks of wolves and night sounds. Only the obvious (but quite unconscious) autobiographical strain of remorse makes the poem noteworthy. Repeatedly the narrator laments the pain of memory: he is unable to forget or escape his past life; sin and guilt are overwhelming realities from moment to moment; nothing, not nature, not will power, not remorse, can release him from the certainty of his responsibility. In *Eliot*, Channing seems obsessed with a remorse for his own past. Perhaps in his old age (he was now near seventy) he was seeing the shambles of his home life. Now the lifetime of optimism seemed unable to protect him against his sense of guilt which was as strong as that in his friend Hawthorne. But the poem fails to bring the themes of guilt and remorse into any coherent pattern. The weight of the blank-verse narrative and the thinness of the language combine to keep the poem in an appropriate obscurity.

IV   John Brown

The last of Channing's work published in his lifetime was *John Brown and the Heroes of Harper's Ferry* (1886), a blank-verse drama that shows the hold Brown had on the New England imagination. Channing had remained indifferent, even hostile, to Brown when the fanatic had visited Concord in 1857 and 1859. This second visit most favorably impressed Emerson, Thoreau, and Alcott; but Channing never was affected by the powerful personal attractiveness Brown radiated. Though he had denounced slavery uncompromisingly in his early poetry and had even voted for the Free-Soil ticket of 1852,[23] Channing had little sympathy with the Abolitionists in general and with Brown in particular. Even more than Thoreau, Channing kept politics and literature separate.

But the memory of the moral fervor of the days before the Civil War was still strong. In 1878, Samuel Orcutt, a Connecticut minister and Alcott's good friend, began a history of Torrington, Connecticut, Brown's birthplace. For the book, Orcutt persuaded Channing to write a poem commemorating Brown. The poet wrote "The Burial of John Brown," which was published in Orcutt's book. Brown, it was clear, was living as a symbol for many in New England just as he had in 1859 personally presented a moral challenge to a select few. Thoreau, for instance, was moved in spite of his own passive resistance. "We have made a subtle distinction," he wrote, "have forgot human laws, and do homage to an idea."[24] In Brown, Thoreau saw in 1859 and Channing in 1878 a moral principle carried into action: here was an act of unquestioned selflessness.

This moral fervor dominates *John Brown and the Heroes of Harper's Ferry*. Above all, the unswerving dedication to a right cause sanctified the events at Harper's Ferry:

> Could not a few, a score, of living souls,
> Mated with one who never was surpassed,
> Go forth into that howling wilderness
> To do or die? and win a hero's grave,
> Leaving the consequence to breed its truth
> In other kindred hearts, whate'er our fates?[25]

No matter that the plan was doomed to failure, nor that the larger political questions of "union splitting" were raised, Brown's was a crusade of virtue: "Perchance our plans may fail for one short hour; / Yet 't is the vast design of God, who leads / A cause to victory by ill precedents, / Failure must prove success!"[26]

But, like the testaments to New England virtue, the poem over-simplifies the emotional and moral questions raised by Brown's highly ambiguous career. Channing has sensitivity neither to the brutal consequences of Brown's actions nor to the horror of fanaticism, and he fails to distinguish between morality and egocentricity. Blinded by his view of Brown's mission, Channing never understands the turmoil the Harper's Ferry raid brought to the nation. As a result, he oversimplifies history and makes distinctions between right and wrong which are too shallow. But his failure is the failure of New England's literature to come to grips with social forces and their relationship to morality made into public action. The heart of Transcendental literature is its meditative questioning and its uncompromising belief in man's capacities. Faced with a John Brown, the Transcendentalists could only affirm or deny, for the ambiguity of morality fused with fanaticism overwhelmed the extensive abilities of Emersonian Idealism.

Brown came to be another of Channing's heroes when he joined Margaret Fuller, Thoreau, and Emerson as representative men for the poet. In them, Channing mirrored the values of friendship among the Concord writers: moral duty, emotional stimulation, and personal integrity. This final narrative poem, like its predecessors, reaches out for more ambitious topics; but it rings hollow because it was thirty years too late. Brown had stirred even Thoreau to public life in the 1850's, but Channing had held ever aloof. Now, only with the passing of the war and with the deaths of most of his literary contemporaries could he give vent to his moral indignation.

Channing rose and fell with the currents of Transcendental energy. A part of a community of imaginative men, he added to the swelling of our literature with his pastoral poems, his assaults on a shabby materialism, and his pleas for emotional vitality. He had written of America's "garden" and of the coming of the "machine," but, when that period of Romantic enthusiasm waned, Channing was helpless to go on alone. He needed his friends; the aggressively self-reliant man was joined irrevocably to the other Concord writers by strong bonds of love and sympathy.

CHAPTER 6

A Perennial Springtime

IN the 1840's Concord had many reputations. It was the center for the Transcendental "nonsense" which was threatening to overcome the enlightened gentility of Boston and Cambridge; it was a mecca for the faithful young people who looked to Emerson for intellectual and moral leadership; it was a gathering place and home for some of the best minds America had been fortunate enough to produce. The physical presence of so many active minds and pens gave rise to a genuine sense of community among these writers. Though dedicated to an ideal of self-development, each in his way lived with his friends and felt himself the more creative for that friendship. At its best, Concord was a center of the American Renaissance, a locale bringing together Emerson, Thoreau, Alcott, Hawthorne, and Margaret Fuller. And, Ellery Channing, too, any one of these writers would have added, for the poet was a respected, integral part of the Concord group. His influence ranged from minor to major, from oblique to direct. He gave hours of freedom to Hawthorne, community to Alcott, inspiration to Margaret Fuller, and genuine friendship to Thoreau and Emerson. If his poetry finally fell short of its promise, his presence more than compensated for that loss. The most arresting of the many paradoxes of Channing's life was the triumph of the role of friend over that of poet.

I *Hawthorne*

No two men were less suited for close friendship than Ellery Channing and Nathaniel Hawthorne: the poet was a Romantic optimist; the novelist, a saturnine skeptic. Channing would sell his prose to the highest bidder, but Hawthorne distrusted and disliked "measured feet and jingling lines."[1] But each had, in his own way, found himself cut off from family traditions; each had

resolutely become a writer only to see his efforts go unrewarded
and little read. Each, in 1843 when Channing settled in Concord,
was recently married, and was freed at last from a paralyzing
emotional isolation. Still, Hawthorne poorly concealed his impatience with Channing's eccentricities ("These originals in a
small way, after one has seen a few of them, become more dull
and common-place than even those who keep the ordinary pathway of life"),[2] but a strange chemistry kept the bond between the
men secure until Hawthorne's death in 1864. Channing frequently
visited the Hawthornes in Salem and Lenox; he cordially welcomed them home after their years in England and Italy. He had
had the additional pleasure of knowing Sophia for a number of
years before her marriage. No matter how diverse the current of
his life from that of the Hawthornes, the two men remained on
good terms.[3]

Channing read Hawthorne's prose more often and more thoroughly than did any of the other Concord writers. Thoreau was
closer intellectually to Hawthorne than was Channing—Hawthorne once wistfully called Channing a poor substitute for Thoreau—but the poet came closer to understanding the significance
of Hawthorne's writing than did either Thoreau or Emerson, each
of whom found fiction superficial. Hawthorne, Channing said,
"had the power to make books like the 'House of Seven Gables,'
and the 'Scarlet Letter,' which showed an original talent such as
very few Americans had. Mr. Emerson did not think so; he never
read Hawthorne. . . ."[4] Channing was so familiar with Hawthorne's
style that he saw Sophia's meddling hand in the *Notebooks* long
before anyone else suspected it. Of the emendations, Channing
told Sanborn: "Mrs. Hawthorne . . . I suppose, connected its frag-
ments together by remarks of her own. When I read it the style
did not seem to be exactly Hawthorne's."[5]

Fiction was not, however, poetry; and Hawthorne lacked that
open enthusiasm for nature that motivated Channing. "Once in
Concord I took him to Gowan's Swamp," said Channing. "It was
a choice walk, to which Thoreau and I did not invite everybody.
When we reached the place Hawthorne said nothing, but just
glanced about him and remarked: 'Let us get out of this dreadful
hole!' "[6] No one who consistently saw "dreadful" holes in nature
could be Channing's closest companion—friendship had obvious
limitations. But Channing had touched Hawthorne's life; for, as

Rose Hawthorne recalled many years later, the moody poet had been welcomed not only by the Hawthorne adults but also by the children. Channing's wit and imagination lingered for good reason in the memories of those who knew him best.

As Hawthorne wrote the introductory essay for *Mosses from an Old Manse,* he recalled with deep pleasure the early days in Concord with Channing. Their favorite pastime had been rowing the Middlesex rivers with no other aim than to enjoy themselves away from the hot, dusty, dull village. Here, freed from routine, Hawthorne escaped the "dead ideas" he had found obsessively present in the Old Manse attic, for he carefully arranged the sketch to contrast the musty, sterile theological tracts with the fresh, spontaneous conversation with Channing. Like each of the other Concord writers, Hawthorne had discovered that an afternoon spent with Channing was not wasted; despite the flights of fancy, the nonsense, the non sequiturs of rambling wit, "lumps of golden thought . . . lay glimmering in the fountain's bed and brightened both our faces by the reflection."[7] Almost with wonder, Hawthorne saw what was inherently sound in Channing: he was intelligent beyond the ordinary man; he was more consistently imaginative than his verse hinted. But all the "gold" lay unused: "Could he have drawn out that virgin gold and stamped it with the mint mark that alone gives currency, the world might have had the profit, and he the fame."[8] This tribute is no mere flight of sentimentality, for memory had kept fresh the luster of Channing's presence. At a time when Hawthorne had been brought back from the "dungeon of the heart" by Sophia, he was shown hours of free imaginative play by Channing.

Freedom, Hawthorne thought, was the gift of those excursions: "The chief profit of those wild days to him and me lay, not in any definite idea . . . but in the freedom which we thereby won from all custom and conventionalism and fettering influences of man on man."[9] Ideas he had found in the Manse where the mind was crabbed and attenuated by the weight of the past and by man's necessity to impose those ideas upon his experiences. The seemingly inconsequential boat rides with Channing helped Hawthorne untangle his life from the Manse; they gave an impetus for his growing mastery over his intellectual material. "We were so free today that it was impossible to be slaves again to-morrow."[10]

Hawthorne was too honest with himself to allow the gleam of

the golden afternoon to blind him to other truths. The Old Manse still stood, ready to receive him home, inevitably to be dealt with: "How gently did its gray, homely aspect rebuke the speculative extravagances of the day!"[11] Channing's influence was confined to the river; he could never understand Hawthorne's concern for human finitude. For his part, Hawthorne could not afford to spend his life on the river because, for him, spontaneity was fleeting; other demands arose after the excursion. With this conscious awareness of Channing's values and limitations for him, Hawthorne found his emotions and his good sense challenged many times. Once, thinking to help his friend in a time of trouble, he considered inviting Channing to stay with him for a few days while Sophia was gone. But, knowing Channing's temper and his own irritability in his wife's absence, Hawthorne wisely dropped the idea by pointedly concluding that Channing "should have been whipt often and soundly in his boyhood; and as he escaped such wholesome discipline then, it might be well to bestow it now. But somebody else may take him in hand; it is none of my business."[12]

The exasperation of a moment was not to be the final memory of a long friendship, for the two never suffered a serious break in their affection. The reserve so characteristic in Channing kept a manageable distance between him and Hawthorne. Not many years before Channing's arrival in Concord, Hawthorne had had to fend off the much warmer emotions of Jones Very, the Salem scholar-mystic who wanted to find Hawthorne a "brother." Hawthorne quickly retreated from the otherwise favorable opinion he held of Very, for he opened himself to no other man on the terms of "brotherhood." Channing, however, kept a seemly distance between himself and Hawthorne; a willing companion for skating, rowing, smoking, or lounging, he scrupulously respected Hawthorne's privacy, intellectual point of view, and emotional freedom.

The comparison between Very and Channing is instructive, for in them the stark contrast throws light on Channing's strongest qualities. Very was both imaginative and intellectually powerful. His poetry shows strengths of thought and craft far beyond Channing's; he was much more attuned to the spiritual enthusiasm characterizing Transcendentalism; but his fervor thrust him on his friends with no reservations. He so challenged the emotional reserve not only of Hawthorne but of Emerson that they ignored his literary accomplishments. Channing's awareness of his own need for independence and privacy kept him from usurping the emotions of his friends. Hawthorne found that his friend's witty conversation and his delight in the natural world worked as a spur to the imagination. One came away from Very shaken and drained from the continual preservation of one's own self in the face of the fiery visions; one came away from Channing with the "lumps of gold"; with the freshened determination to write. We would expect Channing to have made contributions to the lives of Emerson and Thoreau, to Alcott and Margaret Fuller; but to find the delight he gave Hawthorne, or to recall the intense feeling of freedom the novelist took from him, is to recall again the sheer force of personality Channing conveyed. He had a gift of expression well suited to a world of excursions; in his responsiveness to his friends, he was a born companion.

II *Alcott*

Channing's relationship with Bronson Alcott—a man more sympathetic to the poet's values—was more complex and more rewarding for both men. In his first days in Concord, Channing had not been able to take Alcott very seriously. Alcott's Fruitlands experiment, his mystical "Orphic Sayings" in *The Dial,* his association with the English mystic J. P. Greaves, and his friendship with the incomprehensible Charles Lane—all these made Alcott ludicrous to Channing to whom this combination of abstract theorizing and communal living was wholly alien. At best, the comings and goings of this strange group were material for an active sense of humor; the natural excesses of Lane and Alcott were only "making cucumbers of moonshine."[13]

Shortly after he settled in Concord, Channing visited the Alcotts at Fruitlands in 1843; but it was not until 1848, when Emerson was in Europe and Alcott's family was scattered on visits to relatives, that the two, temporarily shorn of their closest companions, developed what was to be a lasting friendship. Through the conversations of long days in the woods, Alcott discovered an unexpected treasure trove in Channing. Once away from Lane, Alcott showed a sensible concreteness: Channing's imaginative talk was matched by Alcott's wide reading; and the instinctive love of rural life in each man provided a community of spirit that allowed common interests to flourish.

From 1848 until Channing moved to New Bedford in 1856, the two were close friends. Alcott often visited Channing; and, in turn, the Alcott home was a frequent way station on Channing's unpredictable excursions. Like Emerson, Ward, and Sanborn, Alcott championed his friend to people less capable of fathoming the peculiarities of a poetic mind. He wrote, for instance, to Sarah Helen Whitman recommending Channing's lecture series to the Providence Lyceum.[14] The role of an intellectual broker came naturally to Alcott because he harbored a life-long ideal of intellectual community. Channing, he quickly saw, added to Concord's stock of intellectual reserve; his presence was to be announced whenever possible.

The first attenuation of the Alcott-Channing friendship grew inevitably from Ellen Channing's death in 1856. Just as Channing was withdrawing into his own world of private tensions, Alcott increased his public conversations and joined the St. Louis Hegelians in a long partnership of lecturing and public symposia. At this time a two-year quarrel began when Channing bluntly criticized a letter Alcott had written to David Wasson, the poet-minister in Worcester. In a typical burst of enthusiasm, Alcott had compared Wasson's sonnets to Shakespeare's. "Channing, on reading my note," wrote Alcott, "cooly [*sic*] advised me to 'burn it,' and I in return commanded him to 'find the door forthwith'— which he did. . . ."[15]

Channing's mercurial temper never showed itself more quickly than when he felt himself insulted. All his earlier disgust with Alcott's exaggerations was suddenly renewed and magnified in this abrupt confrontation. Each man had encroached on the other's emotional territory: Alcott was jealous of his critical perspicuity; Channing was the ever-present gadfly. Channing, whose own exaggerations of personality vie with Alcott's in the minds of later historians as the most pronounced in Transcendental literature, could strike any man from his presence. The Transcendental community was clearly prey to ordinary emotions of pique, jealousy, and frustration. Far from being an insulated group of idealists, these men rubbed edges, irritated and disappointed each other; but they usually had the strength to hold their emotions in check, and to allow reconsiderations to repair the ravages of haste.

This eruption of disharmony between Alcott and Channing ended as abruptly as it had begun when Channing appeared at the Alcotts in 1859 as if nothing had happened to alter their friendship. He became a weekly visitor at the Alcotts where he was on quite cordial terms with Mrs. Alcott who had years of practice in comforting improvident intellectuals. Perhaps more than anyone in the late 1860's and early 1870's, she was the gentle light in Channing's troubled nighttime. "Her table was spread for him twice at least every week, and her afternoons and evening given to him unreservedly," Alcott wrote.[16] Channing often spent the evening talking to her rather than to Alcott. "Whim, thy name is Channing," Alcott wrote in exasperation.[17]

But whims pass. Channing consistently buoyed Alcott by his talk and by his presence as a member of the informal "academy" of thinkers and poets whom Alcott found so necessary. Like almost everyone who knew Channing, Alcott relished his conversation. "Ellery Channing is here today," he wrote in 1853, "and discourses with rare good sense on life, literature, and literary men. And he permits me to open before him my Collections, and dips with me here and there into the same, having the shrewdest suggestions for me as we run over the leaves together. His is a far wiser and wittier mind than most persons are aware of. . . ."[18] Channing clearly was an intellectual equal in Alcott's eyes; he was a man to be sought for "good sense" on the topics most vital to Alcott. Nothing in such an afternoon was trivial; nothing was sycophantic or frustrating. Alcott knew from experience that the number of men who could talk well was limited, and those who could talk well on "life, literature, and literary men" were a select group indeed. Channing's intelligence, quickness, and perseverence were not often found in American life.

For Alcott, conversation was as necessary as breathing. Instead of merely lecturing as Emerson and Thoreau did, he conducted "Conversations" by engaging the audience in a dialogue. "My theory of Conversation as the natural organ of communicating, mind with mind," he wrote, "appears more and more beautiful to me. It is the method of human culture. By it I come nearer the hearts of those whom I shall address than by any other means. I reach the facts of the case."[19] Dialogue for Alcott involved a wide

range of intellectual activity, for in it the whole "soul" was
brought into play. Little wonder that he responded most fully to
those around him who were the most adept conversationalists:
Margaret Fuller, Thoreau, Emerson, and Channing.

Fewer traits are more characteristic of the Transcendentalists
than their admiration for and skillful performance of conversation.
Each knew how to listen; each knew how to respond. Even before
a man wrote, his companions looked for a verbal skill. Does he
speak with originality? force? wit? The pen might falter and
finally fail; but, if the tongue was adept, the man was to be
respected. "Nothing in the world," wrote Alcott in his journal, "is
so rare and precious as this grace of free and elegant discourse;
but it is the late and loveliest flower of all civility, and takes time
to ripen."[20] With his friends, he saw that intellectual life was the
result of hidden laws of conduct, that good talk revealed sympathies and understandings that were central to human experience. "Like magnetism," he wrote in *Concord Days*, "[conversa-
tion] obeys its own hidden laws, sympathies, antipathies, is
sensitive to the least breath of criticism."[21] In short, thought
Alcott, the level and quality of conversation among friends was
an accurate gauge of the quality of life they shared. The more
imaginative and articulate the conversation, the more intense
and rich the life of the speakers. The Concord writers were conscious of this need to talk; they enjoyed it and took satisfaction
by cultivating their conversations. Concord was an "academy" of
talkers as well as thinkers.

Alcott liked Channing's talk more than his writing, finding as
many did, that the formal organization of thought failed to
capture what was most unique in the poet: "Channing's conversation I think far superior to anything of his printed, surpassing
as well in subtlety as compass of thought that of most men I
have known—while his humour, so rarely a talent of this New
England blood of ours, is flushed with an admirable sense, the
more stimulating from the unexpectedness of its caprices."[22]
Alcott exalts a form of intellectual activity that made quick distinctions and judgments. Of the Town and Country Club, for
instance, Channing said with typical verve, "the very name of
the club had been fatal to it; that it promised an impossible
alliance between Boston lawyers, who desired only a smoking-
room, and, on the other hand . . . a number of country ministers,

who expected to be boarded and lodged, and to have their washing done, whenever they came up to the city."[23]

Channing, not only a conversationalist of rare power but also a writer, almost gilded the lily for Alcott who was anxious to see Concord become a literary center because he believed that a writer needed the stimulation of other writers. With an honest sincerity and an unaffected good will, Alcott could write of his friends: "I am the richest of all men in this Commonwealth, I sometimes think, in possessing these friends of mine. I esteem them as the victories of my life. They are country and countrymen. They are lives and places and times, and stand for thoughts and things perennial and enduring."[24] America might lack ruins and traditions, but the mind could grow with such friends; the heart could respond to genuine emotions. Life was full, and the soul liberated in the atmosphere created by writers like Ellery Channing.

The 1853 "Country Walking" manuscript was just the project to warm Alcott's heart. With enthusiasm he recorded the genesis of this book of friendship in his journal: "Emerson read me something lately from a joint production of Ellery's and his which I was glad to know of, and the better pleased at the prospect of its being sometime published."[25] Such a record could not help but publicize the intellectual vibrancy that daily graced Concord. "As elegant and racy as anything in modern literature," Alcott called the book with honest delight and execrable judgment.[26] Not surprisingly, when Alcott paused in 1850 to catalogue the "dozen or twenty persons at most" who constituted the Boston and Concord literary world, he counted Channing with a group including Emerson, Thoreau, Henry Wadsworth Longfellow, James Russell Lowell, and Theodore Parker.[27] Alcott never wavered in his opinion that Channing ranked with the best writers of his generation: "Channing writes better lines of verse than any contemporary, if subtlety and exquisiteness of sense and melody are considered."[28] He could not sustain his performance, Alcott knew, but sudden moments opened up true feeling, pure response.

Taken together, Channing and Thoreau—younger men who evoked Alcott's fatherly emotions—were the "gemini" who, like him, were devoted to rural simplicity. The pastoral theme in Channing's writing appealed intensely to Alcott, who had literally tried to live the life of the "middle ground" during his Fruitlands experiment, and the ardor Channing expresses in his pastoral poetry was an emotion long familiar to Alcott. From a lifetime of reading in Classical literature and from a thorough knowledge of Roman agriculture, Alcott's ideal group sprang from the land. Now in Concord, Alcott thought, he had found the men who came closest to his ideal: "Thoreau has the profoundest passion for the aboriginal in Nature of any man I have known; . . . Channing stands farther from it, yet comes sometimes, in certain moods, as by some happy fate of the moment, into a closer intimacy that makes him passionately one with the heart of things."[29]

Channing's daily habits as well as his verse were exemplary for Alcott: he walked the woods, he shunned the city, he conformed to no man's external ideal. He was ready to share thoughts with Alcott, and he repeatedly celebrated New England in his poetry. Channing's rural ideal found warm sympathy in Alcott, who insisted that "the primitive features of the landscape are being obliterated by the modern facilities for business and travel."[30] Alcott sympathized fully with Channing's loss of imaginative power in the cities. "The town robs me of myself," said Alcott, "while I never return from Nature without spoils that ennoble and fill me."[31]

The rebellion from Boston ran deep in Concord; these children of the Puritans had established an apostate's version of New Jerusalem. The brotherhood of the saints might now be open to all men, but it *was* a brotherhood, and these *were* the elect. Alcott had a strong sense of the distance separating him and his friends from the world surrounding them. "Concord is classic land; for here dwell the poets, the Americans *par excellence* and men of the future, whose names shall render Harvard and Yale, with their professors and halls, one day ridiculous."[32]

Responsive to this sense of community, Channing faithfully supported his friend. Putting aside his hatred of group activity, he was present at the only meeting of the "Concord Club" that Alcott tried to form in 1860. When Alcott solicited manuscripts for a "Concord Book" of writing, Channing gave him poems and encouragement. "Believe me," he wrote Alcott in 1861, "it always gives me great pleasure in any manner to assist you, in any of your literary & social enterprises. . . ."[33] Although the book never appeared, a substitute, *Concord Days,* published by Alcott in 1872, contains three of Channing's poems.

Thoreau, not Alcott, was closest to Channing, but the older man understood perhaps better than anyone how Channing was at the mercy of his caprices and his moody loneliness. In 1857, while visiting Daniel Ricketson in New Bedford, Alcott wrote this analysis of Channing to his wife: "[Channing] seemed saner, & sounder than heretofore when Hillside and its inmates knew him and his caprices untold, if not unendurable. . . . He comes forth from his den to spend the intervals at Woodlawn with his kind friends: sits with Ricketson in his Shanty enjoying his pipe, or strolls with him through the old fields, solitary and sad-seeming through the jocund companionship around him [,] the jubilance of the spring season,—through his own jokes more than all else besides—too fated to weep, or dissolve the frosts of more than forty winters' of Sorrows—wooing the snows forever."[34]

Few men had the ability to see the strengths and weaknesses of a friend that Alcott had. Loneliness, he saw, had formed Channing's youth and harassed his maturity. A queer, obnoxious man to many sensible Concord townsmen, Channing has a mind contoured by the cross currents of strongly conflicting emotions. To Alcott, Channing seemed "fated": he was caught in an inescapable tangle of sorrow over which he had no control, from which he reaped only frustration and disappointment. Unlike Emerson, who had the power to transform sorrow and emotional harrowing into rejuvenating self-control, Channing was brought to an intellectual impasse. Alcott's picture of Channing strolling, isolated from friendship, from nature, and from himself, is strikingly apt. Nothing could penetrate his external manners to reach the inner life, not even his self-consciousness.

Channing had added much to Alcott's own life, Alcott thought; but the poet was essentially a tragic figure whose achievements were always to be neutralized by the "fate" ensnaring him. Always approaching the extraordinary achievement, Channing only occasionally (and often incompletely) crossed the line from intelligence to genius. "The happy fate of the moment," Alcott called those crossings. He saw that the jokes masked a loneliness not to be sounded; he saw that the inner conflicts of insecurity, pugnacity, and willfulness were never to be escaped or mastered.

Years later, after the deaths of Thoreau and Hawthorne, Alcott used his journal to lament the narrowing circle of Concord's literary life. In conclusion, he said of Channing: "Capricious man that [Channing] is, the victim of his moods, whimsical as any spoiled child, and holding his best friends on his own terms or none—may take offense at you know not what, and be off missing for a month, for a twelve-month, unless you take him as he chooses to have you—always walking and talking from behind his mask, and resenting any stroke of candor on your part, as if that were breaking faith with him."[35] The "mask," of course, had to be kept intact by common consent; the first duty of friendship in Concord was to allow each man to define for himself the terms of his own personality before a friend could approach. The mask image (the most accurate description anyone has ever made of Channing) shows the poet's vitality checked by a surface personality. Alcott, regarding Channing and his writings more enthusiastically than did Hawthorne, was more attuned to the poet's point of view toward nature and toward human goodness. Alcott could be more sympathetic than Hawthorne with Channing's wasted potential. Understanding the reasons for the frustration, Alcott appreciated the disaster of a man whose talent was victimized by his inability to step from behind the mask.

This understanding is unique among the Concord writers. Hawthorne was too hostile intellectually; Margaret Fuller was a sister-in-law as well as a friend; Thoreau and Emerson were too sympathetic with Channing to grasp the contradictions in their friend's personality. The responsive chords Channing struck vibrate through Alcott's voluminous journal. Clearly, Channing's presence was to be recorded and applauded. Friendship with Channing had brought Alcott a personal sharpening of the wits throught conversation, a satisfaction that the intellectual community in Concord operated to mutual advantage, and proof that America could and did cultivate poetry. Channing's conversational wit stimulated ideas; the poetry reaffirmed values important to Alcott. In a world often hostile to Alcott's benign optimism, one more poet, friend, and countryman could be counted on for loyalty. As with Hawthorne, an initial set of hostilities became insignificant when faced with a more vigorous, more creative network of influences. The halting, but steady progress is typical of friendship among the Concord writers: many contradictions were first accommodated and then submerged in a strengthened intellectual community.

III *Margaret Fuller*

No other friendship was so troubling and rewarding for Margaret Fuller in its extremes between despair and near-adoration than that with her brother-in-law, for he was at once a cross to bear and a joy. As he increasingly ensnared Ellen in misery, he continued to embody those very attributes Margaret most admired—a love of literature, a devotion to principle, and a prolific pen. Perhaps the extent of the enigma he presented her may be seen in a bit of self-analysis he wrote her during the first few months of his marriage. After cataloguing his faults, he wrote, "Most people would say reform. I say no! Let me have it out. The more faults I have, the harder I must pull, to draw them along the field of life, for they are like to burrs which catch on to everything, & leave a part of themselves where they fixed." Having asserted his self-reliance, Channing concluded: "So I go along. I am tolerably near the surface. My nose at least the tip of it is above water; I breathe the refreshing air of truth, & turn my back on the fishes, who are straining the great waters of trumpery through their gills."[36] Here, Margaret could see, was disaster lurking for her sister. The "burrs" of independence eventually would drag Ellen down, but who could reject one who did breathe the rare air of truth? The independence caught her admiration; a fellow idealist, she accepted Channing's freedom. From this time until her death, she was never to separate the conflicting qualities in him.

When he came into her life as something other than a contributor to *The Dial*, Channing was more than just a brother-in-law. Although Margaret was very much concerned about Ellen's welfare, she saw Channing's wit and intelligence. He quickly created the role of friend as well as of relative. For his part, he welcomed her into his exclusive world. He read her work with enthusiasm; and, while keeping his praise encased in elaborate exaggerations, he let her know that she had affected him deeply. At Emerson's in 1842, while Channing was looking for a house, he composed a sonnet for Margaret which praised her "lofty life that with the angel flies, / And humble love that clasps humanity."[37] That "lofty life" continually impressed, even awed, Channing. He could be the most cynical man in Concord on occasion, but she always drew out his most perceptive and imaginative responses.

Shaken by Margaret's death, almost dazed from the pain of searching for her body, he wrote to his wife urging her accept the death in the same spirit as Margaret had lived. "To noble souls like hers, life & death are not so far divided. And great calamities are to be borne greatly, or else not borne at all. To the noble, to so noble a person as Margaret, all common grief would be but an impertinence. We must reverence the principles by which she lived, & not the manner of her death."[38] The letter then concludes with an unaffected, honest declaration of love for Ellen. Margaret's death had shaken him, cut through the insecurity, and touched the strength of his personality.

Emerson drew from him a similar response showing the impact Margaret had made. "It fitted exactly,—that shipwreck,—thought Ellery, to the life and genius of the person. . . . For goodness is a sad business . . . and, if he was insurer, he would never insure any life that had any infirmity of goodness in it."[39]

In Channing's own loneliness and with his own self-doubts expressed in the impulsively erratic behavior that had tormented Margaret, he had seen a constancy of temper and a genuine love in her. "Every feature of those she loved," he wrote Marcus Spring, her New York friend, "she enlarged & saw them in high & heroic aspect as part of a whole destiny which she alone came courageously to perform."[40]

Of this responsiveness to her friends, Channing had clear right to speak, for he was one of the galaxy of new luminaries orbiting this spectacular woman. From her childhood on, Margaret Fuller attracted young men of talent and intellectual accomplishment; not only Channing, but his cousin William Henry Channing, James Freeman Clarke, Charles King Newcombe, and Sam Ward stood loyally by her. Older men, too—Frederick Henry Hedge, Alcott, Horace Greeley, and Emerson—found in Margaret a challenging combination of genius, emotional energy, and sexual attraction. Reacting acutely to the preposterous but universal notion of feminine shallowness, she seemed determined to reverse centuries of prejudice against women by herself. By his marriage, Channing had found a unique place in this fabric of intellectual and emotional substance. He, unlike the others, was no direct competitor to her. A poet (rather than essayist, critic, or preacher) by vocation and a brother by chance, he stood alone in his relationship to her mind.

Margaret could respond to him, therefore, without the defensiveness that marked her reactions to Alcott or to Emerson. Like all who probed beneath Channing's surface absurdities, Margaret found in him a mind that provoked hers, a set of ideals to assure her. Once, walking together through Cambridge's Mount Auburn Cemetery, the two naturally talked of death and its meaning; later, in her journal, she found her mind moving from Channing's words to fresh speculation. He gave her the opportunity and impetus to think, to test her ideas, and to end the day with the satisfaction of finding her thoughts clarified. With justification she could write, "Ellery & I had a good afternoon at Mt. Auburn."[41]

On a visit to Emerson's home, she was all but dazzled by the quick and suggestive play of Channing's conversation. "Following up the humor of the moment, he arrests admirable thoughts on the wing," she wrote.[42] Channing had for her precisely the right combination of fresh responsiveness and verbal skill. Though he might dart into trivial fancy, he quickly returned to more substantial thought. "Unequal and uncertain . . . but in his good moods, of the best for a companion, absolutely abandoned to the revelations of the moment, without distrust or check of any kind, unlimited and delicate, abundant in thought, and free of motion, he enriches life, and fills the hour."[43] The terms— "unlimited," "abundant," "delicate"—are high praise from her, for they show how sympathetic she found Channing. Her own life had the qualities reflected in her provocative brother-in-law.

Channing came closer than he knew to many of the ideals that gave her life direction. Her writing is filled with sadness and impatience over the wasted potential in so many men. Like her contemporaries, she was repelled by the depth of human waste she saw daily: "Man lives in this world, a stranger to its real life, deluded like the maniac who fancies he has attained his throne, while in reality he is on a bed of musty straw."[44] She had all the zeal of the New England Puritans; she knew no compromise: either a man takes his life in his hands or he resigns himself to futility. Because Margaret understood the necessity of finding a deliberate style of living, she understood Channing's rejection of Boston and his love of Concord's rural simplicities.

Literature, in general, and poetry, in particular, she said, were the expressions of that life worth living. The quality of writing an artist produced mirrored the quality of life he lived. Perhaps no other American critic has been so devoted to the idea that art and life find together their purest expression. She was certain that "poesy was the natural life of the soul."[45] Once, concluding an estimate of the fine arts, Margaret "spoke of life, as the art, of which these all were beautiful symbols."[46]

Those who wrote, then, came closest to living lives of extraordinary fullness. Friends to Margaret Fuller were influences on her through their presence and writing. Repeatedly her friends testified to her need of feeling an influence emanating from those around her: a true friend made an impact, wrought changes in her. They could be "sharers" in life drawing a common strength from each other. Clarke is almost ecstatic in recalling the impression she made: "She gave each to himself, acted on each to draw out his best nature, gave him an ideal out of which he could draw strength and liberty hour by hour."[47] As much as Alcott, she knew the value of friends; she had a keenly developed theory of what one friend added to another.

Conversation was the medium of transfer between friends. "Conversation is my natural element," she wrote. "I need to be called out, and never think alone, without imagining some companion."[48] A remarkably diverse group of men and women could unite in remembering Margaret's conversational ability. Through the comments runs the assertion that only in speech did her mind develop, only in personal contact did the vitality that made her impressive emerge. She gave formal "conversations" in the manner of Alcott; she was never too harried, ill, or depressed to absent herself from an evening of talk. "After all," she wrote, "this writing is mighty dead. Oh, for my dear old Greeks, who talked everything."[49]

By now we have seen that Channing could match her word for word. In him, she found another brilliant talker, one who could share her life and spur her mind. "I wish I could retain Ellery's talk last night," she wrote in her journal. "It was wonderful; it was about all the past experiences frozen down in the soul, and the impossibility of being penetrated by anything."[50] With an obses-

sive sensibility to the inspiration of the moment, she (with Alcott
and Emerson) was attuned as few could be to the depths of
Channing's mind. He quickly showed her where her own limitations were; he went on to provoke her into an analysis of her life.
Channing, who worked from a need to understand his own life,
affected her with his clarity and force.

When, as in Channing, conversational skill was united with a
responsiveness to nature and to a productive pen, Margaret had
found an affirmation of her own faith. She needed a continual
reminder that her devotion to such abstractions as "beauty" and
"truth" were not chimeras whose gleaming lights might prove
illusions. When Channing showed her how poetry could flow from
his life and when he showed her that he had ideals she recognized, Margaret once more was strengthened in her own resolve
to live fully. In a deeply sympathetic comment in her journal, she
confesses her admiration for him:

The dignity of Ellery's aspiration astounds me. It makes my own seem
low & external. What! this soul wandered near me, nay, sought my
friendship, & I recognised it not. There is base metal in me, let me
purify. The statue is partly of gold, but the feet are of clay. Shall the
pure children of Jehovah bow down to it? My mind has ebb & flow: it
often leaves the strand forlorn, & mottled with seaweed & strange abor-
tions of the deep. Ellery's view is as spiritual as Mr. Alcott's. He has a
far finer sense of beauty, with out priggishness or cant. Truly the life of
soul is all to him. May he keep it inviolate as hitherto. . . .[51]

Even though she overestimates his "spirituality," her intense
response couples admiration and introspection. The friend again
calls out the best in her mind; he keeps her alive to a healthy
self-consciousness. In conclusion, she says: "As I read Ellery, my
past life seems a poor excuse for not living: my so-called culture
a collection of shreds & patches to hide the mind's nakedness."[52]
Channing had undoubtedly touched her, but the relationship was
always shaped by her responses to him as a poet and friend. His
marriage had safely set him beyond any sexual competition.
"Whatever he is to others," she wrote, "he has been much to me,
if only by heightening my love for the Ideal. Blessings on his
poetic nature, & artist eye!"[53]

Margaret Fuller had an unswerving devotion to her intellectual
ideals. Even a brother-in-law who was letting her sister suffer

could not efface the image of a true poet and friend. She once expressed an attitude showing the triumph of the woman of ideals over the family protector: "In these principles [ideals] I have confidence so profound, that I am not afraid to trust those who hold them, despite their partial views, imperfectly developed characters, and frequent want of practical sagacity."[54] Margaret's intellectual toughness reflects the best in the American Transcendentalists, for here is the determination to live life fully—one that prompted Emerson to leave the church and Thoreau to go to Walden—and the willingness to look past life's surfaces to less obvious realities. Margaret had found strength in Channing; her death ironically allowed him to see it for once in himself: "There is in each of us so noble & heroic a creature, capable to be serene & prosperous in all fortunes, which however so many times is downcast & unalterably fallen."[55] Neither Channing nor Margaret Fuller would bow to "events"; erratic though his career was, he gave to her a necessary affirmation of the possible vitality of a life well lived.

IV   *Thoreau*

"Friendship" was a familiar topic among the Transcendentalists, for the journals of Emerson and Thoreau repeatedly question the meaning, duties, and satisfactions of friendship. Each wrote an essay publicly announcing an ideal of human contact that each knew to be (at least in part) unattainable; each kept a close watch over his responses; and each came to hold differing but coherent ideas of what a friendship might be. Channing gave each man the opportunity to see his ideals in practice. Sympathetic intellectually and emotionally, accepting a common love of nature, living a life of sincere purpose, Channing was a friend of unusual proportions. In their reactions to him, we may see more clearly what friendship meant to both Thoreau and Emerson. But first we need to understand exactly what friendship was to Thoreau. Then we may go on to Channing's role.

"I could tame a hyena more easily than my friend," wrote Thoreau in 1840. "I contemplate him as a granite boulder. He is material which no tool of mine will work. A naked savage will fell an oak with a firebrand, and wear a hatchet out of the rock, but I cannot hew the smallest chip out of my fellow. There is a character in everyone which no art can reach to beautify or deform."[56]

With typical bluntness and vigor, Thoreau recognizes the unassailable individuality in a friend. Only that quality of man which admits of pure originality counted for him. Yet, like so many of his contemporaries, Thoreau recognized that the claim of friendship necessarily ran contrary to this solidity of character. "The price of friendship is the total surrender of yourself," he wrote; "no lesser kindness, no ordinary attentions and offerings will buy it."[57] In such an attitude lies the paradox fundamental to Transcendental friendship: how, given the uniqueness of the individual, is a man to establish relationships without sacrificing his personality?

Thoreau knew friendship was an ideal state seldom if ever reached by actual people. His journal entries reflect his longing for the rewards of human contact, but his comments are tempered with a persistent recognition that such an ideal friendship was only an abstraction: actual friends of necessity fell short of the ideal. Writing in *A Week*, he pungently distinguishes between the ideal and ordinary friend: "We are dreaming that our Friends are our *Friends*, and that we are our Friends' *Friends*. Our actual Friends are but distant relations of those to whom we are pledged. We never exchange more than three words with a Friend in our lives on that level to which our thoughts and feelings almost habitually rise. One goes forth prepared to say, 'Sweet Friends!' and the salutation is, 'Damn your eyes!' "[58]

Thoreau's attitude, based on the distinction between the ideal and actual friend, is highly ambivalent. Although he recognizes the painfulness of man's limited friendship, he fully sees the possibility of this finite relationship helping him on to a higher form of being. This ascension beyond the limits of any specific friendship comes, Thoreau implies, only because we have had the communion between friends. Having made the first tentative, incomplete steps toward the ideal of friendship with specific friends, Thoreau finds himself transported beyond the limitations to a moment of ideal satisfaction.

This experience is based, both ideally and immediately, on a trinity of love, truth, and trust. "How insufficient is all wisdom without love!" he wrote in 1842. "There may be courtesy, there may be good will, there may be even temper, there may be wit, and talent, and sparkling conversation,—and yet the soul pine for life. Just so sacred and rich as my life is to myself will it be to another. Ignorance and bungling with love are better than wisdom and skill without."⁵⁹ For Thoreau, this quality of love is a full acceptance by each friend of the other's character. Love accepts all blemishes, enigmas, crudities, and outrages lying within an individual. Because friendship uncovers these rough edges of personality, the friend has the greater burden of acceptance.

But despite his enthusiasm, the law of love was not so simple, and Thoreau realized its complexities. In *A Week*, when he was organizing his thoughts on friendship, he showed the relationship between love and truth: "but sometimes we are said to *love* another, that is, to stand in a true relation to him, so that we give the best to, and receive the best from, him. Between whom there is hearty truth, there is love; and in proportion to our truthfulness and confidence in one another, our lives are divine and miraculous, and answer to our ideal."⁶⁰ Such truth demands of each friend an emotional toughness which excludes both sentimentality and cynicism. If friendship is to go beyond a mere social relationship, it must *touch* each man; it must bring an honest sense of responsibility. Like Margaret Fuller, he demands a mutual responsiveness from friendship: "It takes two to speak the truth, —one to speak, and another to hear. How can one treat with magnanimity mere wood and stone? . . . Only lovers know the value and magnanimity of truth, while traders prize a cheap honesty, and neighbors and acquaintance a cheap civility."⁶¹ The adjective "cheap" reeks with scorn because Thoreau's dedication to living fully and consciously excludes any shabby conventionality. Truth between friends demands a rigor: either accept your friend or leave him; any alternative is false because it does not "give the best" to the friend.

Only from love and truth can trust come; therefore, only from friendship can a full development of the individual's potential emerge. "The friend does not take my word for anything," he says, "but he takes me. He trusts me as I trust myself. We only need be as true to others as we are to ourselves, that there may be ground enough for friendship."⁶² This trust becomes the sure sign of friendship; when two are joined together on such a level of acceptance, who can cast them asunder with insignificant moments of inconsistency or ill-manners? Thoreau thus takes up the threads of his own dignity and that of his friend to weave a friendship. His relationship with a friend excludes a passive dependence of one friend on the other by engaging each person in the active role.

To this relationship Thoreau ascribes a specific satisfaction: the friend saves him from a destructive isolation. With all of his self-reliance and his profound understanding of man's relationship to nature, Thoreau kept in view his necessity for a friend: "Nature must be viewed humanly to be viewed at all; that is, her scenes must be associated with humane affections, such as are associated with one's native place, for instance. She is most significant to a lover. A lover of Nature is preëminently a lover of man. If I have no friend, what is Nature to me? She ceases to be morally significant."[63]

The ideal quality in friendship begins to emerge in his belief that this temporal relationship corresponds to a fundamental law of the universe: "It takes place, like vegetation in so many materials, because there is such a law. . . . Men naturally, though feebly, seek this alliance, and their actions faintly foretell it."[64] Even the inevitable disappointment between the ideal and real friend shows Thoreau a relationship between man's world and a more universal reality. "When I have withdrawn and am alone, I forget the actual person and remember only my ideal. Then I have a friend again. I am not so ready to perceive the illusion that is in Nature. I certainly come nearer, to say the least, to an actual and joyful intercourse with her. Every day I have more or less communion with her, *as I think*. At least, I do not feel as if I must withdraw out of nature. I feel like a welcome guest. Yet, strictly speaking, the same must be true of nature and of man; our ideal is the only real. It is not the finite and temporal that satisfies or concerns us in either case."[65] This final tribute to the ideal that is superior to the real friendship typifies the Transcendental tension between living relationships and a higher form of "Being" lying beyond corporeal forms. More than Emerson, Thoreau responded to this tension and, while not surrendering to either pole of the paradox, strove repeatedly to accommodate himself to the necessity of friendship while keeping open the possibility of finding an ideal fulfillment.

His journal entries are marked by a tone of longing for human contact, but they are balanced by a deep suspicion of triviality or betrayal. From his early entries to his late ones, Thoreau rarely allows himself to express his longing without qualification. He held himself to a rigorous standard of conduct through the re-examinations in the journal. He raised again and again the hard, but necessary questions: Can the friend *in*-form? Does the friend call out my best, not my second best? Must I make shabby concessions to my friend's feelings? Have I demanded too much? The questions persist in his mind because Thoreau had found in abstemiousness a touchstone of living. But his relationships with his friends drew him away from his austerity by the very longing to which he was responding. He was finding values which enlivened and threatened at the same time. Here were not only love, trust, and sympathy but also self-indulgence, flattery, and triviality. The journal records Thoreau's life-long attempt to be a friend without sacrificing his austere dignity. He consciously develops his ideal against his experience without becoming either cynical or despondent. This, then, is Thoreau's ideal state of Friendship, we can now begin to understand how important was his specific friendship with Ellery Channing.

Perry Miller, who explored Thoreau's idea of friendship in *Consciousness in Concord,* finds Thoreau victimized by a perverse egoism. "The story is painfully clear, interpret it how one will," says Miller: "from the beginning Thoreau's frantic concern with the idea of friendship is a struggle to make it perverse, to make it a judgment on the faults of friends, to equate it with hatred."[66] A "perfervid cult" Miller calls this friendship among the Concord friends, for he sees a powerful impulse to use friendship as a subtle means of torment. Miller even accuses the friendship of being a device "for being let down by their friends—so that the friends could then be accused of cowardice."[67] Miller is correct in seeing the astringent, even hostile emotions lying amid the enthusiasm of Transcendental friendship; but what he ignores is the way these people accommodated and even used this ambivalence to triumph finally over their very limitations. Surely Channing was for Thoreau a cross to bear because of his petulance; surely Thoreau saw in him an opportunity to vent his hostilities; but Channing was much more than a convenient clawing post on which Thoreau sharpened his wit. Miller's analysis gives, therefore, but half the necessary understanding of the Transcendental attitude toward friends.

Thoreau was close, very close, to Channing for twenty years in spite of the wrangles and tempestuous outbursts. The rank, fetid hatred Miller describes simply was not motive enough to sustain this friendship (nor does it account for the sense of community drawing all the Concord writers together). More fundamentally, Channing came closer than any other person to reconciling the paradox of friendship for Thoreau.

As McGill has shown, the two shared public disrepute in Concord. Each was an eccentric individualist who took obvious delight in rubbing against the grain of the town's expectations. Neither would work steadily; neither paid much attention to his family; both were commonly thought to be lazy.[68] But beyond external similarity lay a bond of affection which went deeper, for Thoreau found in Channing a man capable of giving and receiving "love": "[to] give the best to, and receive the best from." Channing admired Thoreau so deeply that he demanded nothing from his friend but a fundamental ease and naturalness. Moreover, few men understood Thoreau's love of nature as Channing did. As we have seen in *Thoreau: The Post-Naturalist*, Channing accurately assessed his friend.[69] From such an understanding could come sympathy and trust. Only in the presence of a man attuned to his own deepest ideals could Thoreau begin to find a "Friend."

The inner tensions that shaped Channing's personality gave him fortuitous hesitancy and emotional reservation. He cared nothing for the politeness of manners, for flattery, or for the usual superficial attentions that pass for friendship. His "mask" that puzzled Alcott created an emotional distance between him and Thoreau. Channing—for all his wit and talk—was a shy man who would not parade his emotions cheaply in front of his friends. When Thoreau thought of a friend, he thought of a man who had just that "rind" that encased Channing: "Love is a thirst that is never slaked. Under the coarsest rind, the sweetest meat. If you would read a friend aright, you must be able to read through something thicker and opaquer than horn."[70] Poetry, not his friendships, was Channing's outlet for his emotions. He could therefore approach Thoreau on his friend's terms.

Thoreau calls this harmony "love"; he calls it "sympathy." The two men had such a sympathy as comes from inner, not trivial, harmony. Each had turned his back on the familiar world of society to find himself in a world of nature because each had visions of man's potential. Not caprice, not whim, but imagination had caused each man to look for resources of independence. For instance, they walked together. Seemingly this similarity is a trivial one to be expected from residents of a village in rural New England, but Thoreau knew that the companion of a walk could make the difference between wasted time and revelation: "I know of but one or two persons with whom I can afford to walk. With most the walk degenerates into a mere vigorous use of your legs, ludicrously purposeless, while you are discussing some mighty argument, each one having his say, spoiling each other's day, worrying one another with conversation, hustling one another with our conversation."[71] Channing, one of the two of whom Thoreau alludes in this journal entry, did not spoil the day; he brought the trust (and love and truth) Thoreau demanded. Thoreau, of course, was uncommonly serious about his walks. "Every walk," he says, "is a sort of crusade, preached by some Peter the Hermit in us, to go forth and reconquer this Holy Land from the hands of the Infidels."[72] The imagery is instructive: Thoreau and Channing were a pair of knights in homespun who were living with a religious intensity. To be a friend in this sense was to share the holy imperative.

The quotations from Channing's conversations that Thoreau carried to his journal show how close the two men were in mind (and in verbal ability, for here Channing's mind is freed of the limitations that dogged his poetry). About walks in the woods, Channing said, "You don't want to discover any-thing new, but to discover something old."[73] He knew as well as Thoreau that mere originality was meaningless; what each was after in nature was a truth defying time—a truth with the sanctity of permanence. On what men *needed* for life (as opposed to the meretricious goals most common) Channing could take his satisfaction exactly as Thoreau did. "The stars are few and faint," wrote Thoreau after a moonlit walk with Channing. "How well they wear! C. thought a man could still get along with *them* who was considerably reduced in his circumstances, that they were a kind of bread and cheese that never failed."[74] Thoreau, Concord's self-appointed inspector of snow storms, approved of Channing's definition of winter as "the sabbath of the year. The perfect winter days are cold, but clear and bright."[75] Because he was intensely aware of his isolation in his love of nature, Thoreau could take a unique pleasure in a footprint, as when he had taken an acquaintance on a winter walk: "We came upon the tracks of a man and dog, which I guessed to be Channing's. Further still, a mile and a half from home, as I was showing to T. under a bank the single flesh-colored or pink apothecium of a baeomyces which was not covered by the snow, I saw the print of C.'s foot by its side and knew that his eyes had rested on it that afternoon."[76] This simple, apparently trivial scene symbolizes the sympathy between Thoreau and Channing. Here was more genuine "love" between human beings in absence than most men find in a lifetime of more conventional experience. So long as Thoreau could respond to Channing's sympathy (here expressed by inspecting the flower), the friendship had "in-formed" him.

Not only the sympathy but the less attractive side of Channing came to make the friendship strong. Channing was becoming proverbial in Concord: if unpredictable behavior was a mark of genius, then he had true genius. The more Channing showed his independence, the more Thoreau could respond to his individuality. The two could keep their differences open between them and thus pass another of Thoreau's tests of friendships. He was careful to keep Channing's failures in mind as if to test the virtue of truth. "C. is one who will not stoop to rise," Thoreau writes. "He wants something for which he will not pay the going price. He will only learn slowly by failure,—not a noble, but disgraceful, failure."[77] This criticism gave Thoreau a specific test of his attitude toward Channing and toward friendship. Only through such honesty did his friendship have meaning, so he self-consciously held himself and Channing to his ideal.

Thoreau also recognized the boor in Channing: "Two young men who borrowed my boat the other day," wrote Thoreau in his journal, "returned from the riverside through Channing's yard, quietly. It was almost the only way for them. But, as they passed out his gate, C. boorishly walked out his house behind them in his shirt-sleeves, and shut his gate again behind them as if to shut them out. It was just that sort of behavior which, if he had met with it in Italy or France, he would have complained of, whose meanness he would have condemned."[78] The simon-pure Channing, thought Thoreau, could complain about foreign hostility and then turn around and be obnoxious. But still, to see that in his friend became a touchstone. Struck against such an abrasive act, did the friendship show brass? No, it showed honesty and recovery. Friendship, like all of life's experiences, demanded from Thoreau self-analysis. Without the consciousness of that analysis with its deliberation and its weighing, no relationship was of value. If, as Miller so strongly says, this consciousness sacrificed spontaneous emotion, then Thoreau willingly paid the price and lived to see that it was not a pyrrhic triumph.

Thoreau's stringent analysis of his friend brooks no illusions. So long as Thoreau could recognize the weaknesses in Channing, he could keep himself free of the sentimentality he so feared. He had, of course, a mind capable of holding complexities of personality clearly in view. To Emerson, Thoreau wrote with amusement of Channing's unpredictable bursts of fancy:

He also goes often to Alcott's, and confesses that he had made a discovery in him—and gives vent to his admiration or his confusion in characteristic exaggeration—but between this extreme & that you may get a fair report—& draw an inference if you can. Sometimes he *will* ride a broomstick still—though there is nothing to keep him or it up— but a certain centrifugal force of whim which is soon spent—and there lies your stick—not worth picking up to sweep an oven with now. His accustomed path is strewn with them. But then again & perhaps for the most part he sits on the Cliffs amid the lichens, or flits past on noiseless pinion like the Barred Owl in the daytime—as wise & unobserved.[79]

Thoreau had little use for the broomstick, but the owl he saw in his own soul. The ability to see Channing as he described him to Emerson is a demonstration of Thoreau's idea of harmony between friends that preserves and strengthens each man so that "in silence they will digest [common themes] as one mind; but they will at the same time be so two and double that each will be to the other as admirable and as inaccessible as a star."[80]

The silence of the owl in Thoreau's description of Channing was of special value to him for whom a well-timed silence was as revealing as conversation. "Not that [my companion—Thoreau's favorite term for Channing] can tell a good story," he wrote, "but that he can keep a good silence. Has he attended to a silence more significant than any story?"[81] Channing knew when to watch and when to speak; conversation between him and Thoreau was of the sort to enhance the excursion. "Words should pass between friends as the lightning passes from cloud to cloud," Thoreau wrote. "I don't know how much I assist in the economy of nature when I declare a fact. Is it not an important part in the history of the flower that I tell my friend where I found it? . . . We wish to spread and publish ourselves, as the sun spreads its rays; and we toss the new thought to the friend, and thus it is dispersed."[82] For twenty years, Channing humanized nature for Thoreau by being the friend to whom thoughts could be tossed, and thus was trust made concrete in the lives of two friends. Because their friendship had created such a trust, Thoreau knew he could be open with Channing, that his friend would understand his love of nature, his mysticism, and his revulsion toward society. By experience, Thoreau had found that with Channing he could be "simple and unconstrained," an ultimate test of friendship.

Through his friendship with Channing, Thoreau found his principles of friendship made concrete. The intensity of the relationship was a daily test for Thoreau of the worth of his speculations about man's life with his fellows. He so distrusted abstractions that the frequent contact with Channing gave him a way to experience his ideals. More than anyone else, Channing kept Thoreau alive to human sympathy without diverting him from his "self-exploration." Channing gave as much as he demanded, for he shared deeply held values. He uniquely made friendship a living experience for Thoreau to whom no values were real until they were lived.

V *Emerson*

Emerson's attitudes toward friendship differed from Thoreau's in degree and emphasis. For both, love and sincerity were necessary; both recognized friendship as a pathway to an ideal world, but where Thoreau's intensity is reserved for this ideal state, Emerson concentrates on the effect friendship had on the individual personality. His point of view is well defined by the final lines of the poem he prefixed to his essay "Friendship." In this poem he uses images of a mill round and of fountains to capture the metamorphosis and renewal which transform the drudgery of daily routine into sparkling life as the long-hidden recesses of individuality are exposed.[83] The poem's emphasis is action: friendship acts, and man is ennobled. For Emerson, friendship becomes a process whose end is freedom.

The essay itself exalts the self-reliance which friendship brings. "The soul environs itself with friends," Emerson writes, "that it may enter into a grander self-acquaintance or solitude; and it goes alone for a season that it may exalt its conversation or society."[84] True to his life-long code of ethics, Emerson keeps central the possibility of spiritual development. His feeling of coldness and his suspicion of being distracted by his friends from life's essentials find solace in the paradox that each friend brings more than he takes.

Only the highest form of integrity keeps this process from becoming spiritual vampirism. The strength of character, the most rugged individualism makes a person a worthy friend. "Let him not cease an instant to be himself," Emerson asserts in "Friendship." "The only joy I have in his being mine, is that the *not mine* is *mine.* . . . Better be a nettle in the side of your friend than his echo."[85] Emerson distrusts people who mimic those stronger, more highly developed personalities in whose orbit they move. He prefers roughness, acidity, and bluntness to fawning imitation. Friendship's just claim is integrity: "Of course, these people, these and no others, interest us,—the dear and beautiful beings, who are absorbed in their own dream. . . . Any other affection between men than this geometric one of the relation to the same thing is a mere mush of materialism."[86]

This union of two strong natures—which for him, as well as for Thoreau, is "of one web with the laws of nature and of morals"[87]— adds to personal growth. From a less developed individuality, the partners of a friendship rise to higher forms of personality: "the object of this intercourse is, that a man may be made known to himself to an extent that in solitude is not practicable. Our faculties are not called out except by means of the affections."[88] Unlike Thoreau's mystical Transcendence, Emerson's ideal is a more attainable individual development. Even more consistently than Margaret Fuller, Emerson tests a friendship by its effect. "We act for, with, upon each other," he wrote. "Our duty our necessity is continually forcing us into active relations with others."[89] Stung at being chastised by his friends for coldness, Emerson explored friendship as the release from such emotional isolation.

Conversation, he found, was the first and most attractive fruit of genuine friendship. "What sorrow it would be," he wrote in his journal, "if in this our mediterranean life where griefs & inconveniencies breed thick as caterpillars we could not *talk.* . . . The way to bereave life of its vulgarity & its barbarism is to celebrate by *Conversation* the sweet & solemn marriage of Reason & Affection."[90] Emerson added his voice to the praise of verbal activity that consistently drew him to his friends. The formal "conversations" of Alcott and Margaret Fuller had their local, daily counterparts in Concord. Through talk, Emerson found the soul stirred, the emotions thawed: "The office of conversation is to give me self-possession. I lie torpid as a clod. Virtue, wisdom, sound to me fabulous,—all cant. I am an unbeliever. Then comes by a safe and gentle spirit who spreads out in order before me his own life and aims, not as experience, but as the good and desirable. Straightway I feel the presence of a new and yet old, a genial, a native element. . . . I regain, one by one, my faculties, my organs. . . . The effect of the conversation resembles the effect of a beautiful voice in a church choir. . . ."[91]

The blessings of these moments of fraternal communion are brief, transient, and elusive; but, thought Emerson, they were worthy of a true literature could they be arrested. Ruminating on a particularly stimulating visit by Alcott, Emerson wrote: "I would rather have a perfect recollection of all this, of all that I have thought & felt in the last week, than any book that can now be published."[92] Emerson knew well that these conversations could thrive only through spontaneity, yet he refused to let this evanescence obscure their worth for him: "The value of the conversation is not measured according to the wisdom of the company but by quite other & indefinable causes, the fortunate moods. I think we owe the most recreation & most memorable thoughts to very unpromising gossips."[93]

Channing used his ability to talk well as an entrance into Emerson's life. Channing was a friend whose conversation enlivened countless hours in the woods, a friend whose "poetic eye" not only graced an afternoon but released a flow of creativity in Emerson himself. Wit, the sure sign of a lively mind and an active imagination, was securely fixed in Emerson's catalogue of values. "E[llery] laughed at Nuttall's description of birds," Emerson wrote. " 'On the top of a high tree the bird pours all day the lays of affection,' etc. 'Affection!' [said Channing] 'Why, what is it? A few feathers, with a hole at one end, and a point at the other, and a pair of wings; Affection! Why, just as much affection as there is in that lump of peat.' "[94] Such a quick-witted observation helped preserve nature from sentimentality and kept Emerson

aware of the power of conversation. "What a climate!" Channing
burst out. "One day they take the cover off the sun, and all the
Irishmen die of drinking cold water; and the next day you are up
to your knees in snow."[95] Emerson knew the value of joy; he knew
the feeble hold most men have on their lives, so that any such
expression of spontaneity as Channing's was more than entertain-
ment: it was proof of a life lived fully. "Eloquent, affectionate,
practical," Emerson concluded, "wise tongues hold society together, move it about, & are worth all the rest of our pleasures &
powers."[96]

But Channing's conversation was more than apothegms and
repartee when he turned to nature's beauty. Once, recently home
from Cape Cod, Channing could show Emerson how much the
summer resident, the lazy urban man, missed on the Cape. The
desolate beauty of that deserted beach was overpowering. "There
is a solitude which you cannot stand more than ten minutes,"[97]
Channing told Emerson, thereby making himself welcome for his
perceptiveness. "In walking with Ellery," said Emerson, "you
shall always see what was never before shown to the eye of
man."[98] Emerson was alert to new views of his familiar world.
Channing, who took their walks seriously, showed his friend unexpected sights. "The *mikania scandens*," wrote Emerson, "the
steel blue berries of the cornel, the eupatoriums, enriched now
and then by a well-placed cardinal, adorned the fine shrubbery
with what Channing called judicious, modest colors, suited to the
climate, nothing extravagant, etc."[99] Few men shared a set of
values with Emerson that would allow for an afternoon of flowers
and cardinals; few men, furthermore, gave Emerson the satisfaction Channing gave. Many might walk with him, but few saw as
much as Channing; fewer still could make the change so deftly
and vigorously from sight to conversation. For all of his own
powers of observation, Emerson repeatedly found that Channing
could call attention to new colors and forms. The ever-present
abstraction "beauty" came alive and was made concrete by Channing's presence.

On a boating excursion, Channing startled Emerson with the
quickness of his eye. "As for beauty," Channing told him, "I need
not look beyond an oar's length for my fill of it." Sure enough,
Emerson recorded in his journal, there was something new: "I do
not know whether he used the expression with design or no, but

my eye rested on the charming play of light on the water which he was striking with his paddle." Because of Channing's casual remark, Emerson beheld hues, transparencies, and motions that drenched the sensibilities. "I fancied I had never seen such color, such transparency, such eddies; it was the hue of Rhine wines, it was jasper and verd antique, topaz and chalcedony; it was gold and green and chestnut and hazel in bewitching succession and relief without cloud or confusion."[100] Judging from the number of such afternoons recorded in the journals, Emerson often used Channing's eye.

This anecedote about beauty concludes a longer passage in the journal which begins with an exasperated analysis of Channing's habits as a poet. Emerson found no plan, no movement of the mind in the poetry. Moods were a "natural flow," but quite incomplete. Emerson's juxtaposition of Channing's impotence and creativity is typical and matches reports of his other friends. But more revealingly, this passage sheds light on some of Emerson's attitudes: he clearly preferred a perceptive eye to a finished poem from Channing. He would ignore the crudities of verse for the splendor of conversation. "Sensibility is all," wrote Emerson in 1862 when he again described an afternoon with Channing. "The poorest place has all the real wealth of the richest as soon as Genius arrives. How magical the poor pond under Channing's eyes. . . . From our boat in Walden Pond we saw the bottom at great depth, the stones all lying covered with moss or lichen as they looked of a greenish gray colour. Ellery said, 'There is antiquity, how long they have lain there unchanged.' "[101] Channing demonstrates the "sensibility" in such remarks and shows in them the responsiveness to verify true genius for Emerson who, without hesitation, applauded creativity in any form.

From this friend Emerson sought and found a psychic and esthetic ferment whose exhilaration was endless. He found in Channing not ideas, but sight; he went to the poet for the excitement of seeing responsiveness in action, not for theories. To Margaret Fuller, Emerson could write with complete satisfaction that "I have very pleasant Saturdays with Ellery quite punctually now for a long time. He is & remains the best company, is always superior & inexplicable, and I at least cannot listen to his grave & gay sense without believing that one who overlooks men & things so unerringly, must one day report his opinions as masterly."[102]

The sanguine conclusion is less important to Emerson than the emotional quickening he had been accustomed to finding in Channing.

This admiration sprang in Emerson, as it did in Thoreau, from an unfeigned sympathy with Channing. Again to Margaret, Emerson tacitly acknowledged the frustration Channing had brought her as a brother-in-law, but he then evaluated Channing's relationship to himself: "I could only wish he were born as much for his own happiness, & for yours, as he is for mine. To me, he is, from month to month, from year to year, an incomparable companion, inexhaustible even if it be, & more's the pity, the finest luxury, rather than a necessity of life."[103] The "luxury" here is a symbolic affirmation for Emerson who, like Margaret, needed examples of how his ethics could be lived. Channing the poet, the man of genius, the exemplary companion, was a perpetual demonstration that life was yet to be lived, that we Americans could still free ourselves spiritually and esthetically. "A perpetual holiday," Emerson called him admiringly.[104] With the "wit and love" he found in Channing's friendship, Emerson found his own creativity swelling; luxurious holidays made the necessary workdays more spontaneous.

Just as Margaret Fuller was spurred in developing ideas she had discussed with Channing, Emerson made the transition from recording a conversation with his friend to an elaboration and clarification of the ideas they had touched upon. One conversation with Channing about religion prompted Emerson to think through a scathing critique of Christian mythology concluding with a description of Jesus as that "poor Jewish boy."[105] These repeated contacts with Channing caused the growth in Emerson that he demanded from friendship.

Not by chance did Emerson repeatedly turn to metaphors of painting and of artists to describe Channing because, as we have seen, Channing had an unusual "eye" for form and color. He could call Emerson's attention to those common sights in the woods that would have escaped even the unusual attentiveness of his companion. With his verbal skill, this perception could be communicated with force and imagination; and Emerson would meditate about what he had seen and experienced: "And yet for how many ages of lonely days has that pretty wilderness of White Pond received the sun and clouds into its transparency, and woven each day new webs of birch and pine, shooting into wilder angles and more fantastic crossing of these coarse threads, which, in the water, have such momentary elegance."[106] White Pond, but one of the many ponds in Middlesex County, became new in color and form through Channing's guidance. Here, human responsiveness, imagination, and sympathy merged in a specific experience; here is Emerson's beauty that approaches virtue made concrete through the office of Channing's friendship. The poet had made acquaintance grow into friendship. Little wonder that Emerson could say that "in able conversation we have glimpses of the Universe, perceptions of the soul's omnipotence but not much to record."[107] With Emerson, as with Thoreau, Margaret Fuller, and Alcott, friendship with Channing had hidden his feet of clay in the dazzling light of performance. "Strict conversation with a friend," wrote Emerson, "is the magazine out of which all good writing is drawn."[108] Channing kept the powderhouse dry and full.

Emerson was conscious not only of his need for friends but also of his inadequacy in meeting them on terms of genuine affection. The defensive correspondence between him, Margaret Fuller, and Caroline Sturgis shows how painfully aware he became of the limitations in friendship. But the urge for those particular satisfactions of friendship remained: "I find in my platoon of contrasted figures; as, my brothers, and Everett, and Caroline, and Margaret, and Elizabeth, and Jones Very, and Sam Ward, and Henry Thoreau, and Alcott, and Channing. Needs all these and many more to represent my relations."[109] Of these friends, Channing was uniquely the poet for Emerson; for Margaret and Caroline were women whose sexuality impinged on more rarified emotions; Elizabeth Hoar and William Emerson were relatives (she, at least spiritually, was a sister); Jones Very had been the personification (too literally, at last) of God in man; Thoreau and Alcott were philosophers; and Ward was a critic.

Channing alone was a poet purely and consistently. Of necessity, Emerson thought, Channing called out special requirements as a friend. He needed, and Emerson gave him money, encouragement, introductions to publishers, and unstinting, unhesitating sympathy. In return, Channing brought Emerson the realization that poetry was being written, that the American life was now actively producing poetry that loved nature and held up ideals of

conduct foreign to State Street. Neither money nor bland orthodoxy motivated this poet; here was testimony to individual creativity, to love and beauty no matter how impressionistic the verse.
"Ellery has been prolific of good verses," Emerson typically wrote,
"and showed me many which would content & delight every
gentle soul that was not an Editor. A true poet that child is, and
nothing proves it so much as his worst verses: sink or swim,—hit
or miss, he writes on, & is never responsible."[110] In spite of the
impressionistic vagueness of Emerson's report—a characteristic
response to Channing's poetry—it displays the satisfaction he
found in poetry that came from honest sources, that touched honest emotions.

Channing's friendship with Emerson and Thoreau answers at
least partially the paradox of friendship and self-reliance in the
thought and lives of the Transcendentalists. Each man deeply
respected the claims of friendship; each knew quite consciously
that it brought balance and depth to life; each shows a hidden
fear of isolation not apparent in other pages of the journals and
essays. But with this acceptance of friendship came a deeply
rooted qualification: the integrity of the self was such that even
legitimate claims were to be met only painfully. Thoreau looked
beyond the friend to the *Friend;* Emerson looked for a strengthening of his own power. This irreconcilable tension was met most
successfully through Channing, for he reinforced the satisfactions
of friendship without threatening either of his friends. He offered
much through his love of nature, his conversation, and his tact as
a companion, but he never tried to deflect his friends from their
chosen paths.

VI   *The Nobler Form*

These two friendships that Channing formed also show the
limitations of "Transcendental friendship" because the qualities
which made Channing a superior friend were those that inhibited
and frustrated his family life and his writing. The hours and days
spent in the woods or at Cape Cod or in Canada added to the
burden thrust on Ellen and the children. The frustrations of
poverty, of ragged tempers, and of dulled patience drove Channing out of the house and increased his dissatisfaction with family
life. The claims of friendship with Emerson and Thoreau were
paid with other, equally valid claims on the father and husband.

Emerson and Thoreau encouraged the development of Channing's individuality, but the poet was not strong enough to keep his role of friend balanced against the role of husband.

The temptations of irresponsibility are inherent in Emerson's and Thoreau's writing on friendship, though each knew the protections against such a supine egotism: self-respect and an honest recognition of duty. Channing lacked the self-knowledge which would have led him to strike a more equitable balance between home and woods, but his domestic failure did not lessen his impact on his friends. "Society affects to estimate men by their talents," Thoreau wisely observed, "but really feels and knows them by their characters. What a man does, compared with what he is, is but a small part. To require that our friend possess a certain skill is not to be satisfied till he is something less than our friend. Friendship should be a great promise, a perennial springtime."[111]

To each man according to his need Channing brought unique gifts, and from each he took a very large measure of comfort and encouragement. Truly this was a vigorous set of relationships, for neither the Concord group nor Channing could have been the same without each other. He was a man who acted directly on their lives; for, far from being a sweet and gentle nonentity, he could not be evaded: either one took Channing into his life, or one ignored him forever and thus lost his gifts. His unique individualism guaranteed response to his different moods and talents.

With him, his friends found their theories of friendship, love, genius, and poetry brought into immediate, familiar experience. Above all, daily life and creative genius could not be separated by these men and women; for life and art were genuine only when experienced together. Channing was thus the more rewarding for them. His talk dazzled; his perceptions encouraged; his poetry moved them: in specific ways, he made daily life intellectual and esthetic for his friends. Repeatedly, he did for them what he could not do for himself—he called forth genuine poetry. The movement of a ripple, the greenness of a fern, the notes of a wood bird passed through the alembic of his conversation. Even the obvious disparity between imaginative talk and mediocre verse showed his friends that the life being lived was more genuine than the abstractions of mere literary performance.

In Channing, Thoreau and others found another self-reliant individualist who, though he might run against their grain on occasion, was determined to find and develop his unique *self*. He could at once confirm their faith in the individual and satisfy a strong need for companionship. Even the most determined of self-reliant men in Concord found pleasure in Channing's company. The impossible gulf of love and individualism was bridged through this friendship.

The friendships, too, had a broader meaning for each of the Concord writers (save perhaps Hawthorne). At a time of intense national insecurity about the life of the mind, Channing symbolized the "young American poet." To encourage him and to find delight in his poetry were to promote and to discover esthetic possibilities in what was commonly assumed to be a literary desert. In 1840 (until 1855), *all* the intellectual models and standards available to Margaret Fuller, to Alcott and Emerson, were English or European; but nothing was more common in Concord than the American demands and hopes for a national literature. The fact that Channing persevered, that he was responsive to nature, made his friendship the more significant. "The world is reckoned by dull men a dead subject, whilst it is quick and blazing," wrote Emerson. "Channing, who writes a poem for our fields begins to help us. That is construction, and better than running to Charlemagne and Alfred for subjects."[112] Friendship fueled this blaze; it raised America toward real poetry.

After all, thought Concord, who else wrote poetry? Bryant was timid; Poe, perverse. Longfellow was only a pale European reproduction. Only Lowell (before 1855 and Whitman after) showed promise to rival Channing. It was neither a lack of taste nor blind stubbornness that led Emerson to name Channing "the best poet we have."[113] Ignoring his own poetry (which Channing never matched in quality), Emerson saw in Channing a "poet for poets." The friendship extended Channing by his Concord contemporaries shows how passionately they wanted a truly American record of experience. In these men, friendship weaves together public responsibility and private gratification. Friendship had climbed many stairs: companionship, inspiration, national pride. In these writers and their relationships to Ellery Channing exists a memorable record of how a genuine intellectual community understood itself.

CHAPTER 7

The Casual Transcendentalist

THOREAU spent an evening in 1858 listening to Channing give a lecture at the Concord Lyceum on "Society." Later in the night, he concluded that the lecture had been "all genius, no talent."[1] Critics since then have rightly regarded the comment as a summary of Thoreau's attitude toward his friend's whole career, but they have failed to see that Thoreau was wrong. He assumed that Channing lacked only the art of selection and organization—that only an inattention to the craft of composition stood between Channing and his audience. Nor was this assumption unique to Thoreau, for Emerson had shared it since the days he had first read Channing's poetry. "If I could write as well as you," said Emerson to Channing in exasperation, "I would write a great deal better."[2]

What Channing's friends never understood was the fact that he did *not* share their faith in an ideal world of the spirit. They worked from a belief in "genius" that was inspiration, that intuitively grasped the moral law of the universe. Recognizing in Channing so many of the values they shared—a love of nature and self-reliance, a rebellion from technology, and a veneration of man's emotional life—they assumed a metaphysical belief that Channing seldom exhibits in his writing. Without that motivation, his lack of "talent" was all but inevitable. Language was to him neither the elaborate system of correspondence that it was to Emerson nor the vehicle for making concrete man's understanding of nature that it was to Thoreau.

Channing's lack of precise, inventive figures of speech comes, therefore, directly from his assumption that the poet's duty is to testify to the reality of emotion. His genius led him ever inward, never outward; and he wrote the only kind of poetry he could, given his view of man. The comments of both Emerson and

Thoreau have led later critics to assume that, if Channing had only been careful enough to revise his poetry, he would have been a successful poet. The reality is, however, different: his verse did exactly what he intended—it announced his reactions, emotions, and intellectual beliefs.

In assessing his performance as a poet, we must recognize the limitations of his language, for the lackluster metaphors and images and his routine descriptions too often rob the poems of that imaginative vitality we expect in a poem. Too often Channing is thrown back on vague abstractions and murky phrases. Unlike Emerson and Thoreau, Channing was never alive to the possibilities of symbolism nor to the joy of using language in fresh, precise ways. Added to this limitation are the techniques that so often fail him: he inverts words for rhymes that become strained; he adds to and takes feet from his lines in an erratic, obtrusive attempt to avoid monotony. Channing was a champion of freedom in verse, but his poems show a consistent deference to established practices (sonnet form, blank-verse monologue) and rhythms (the lines are most often iambic stresses in four- and five-beat groups). In this respect, Channing's poetry is little different from the bulk of that written in America before the publication of *Leaves of Grass*. Neither Poe nor Longfellow nor Emerson nor Thoreau had freed himself from regular metric forms or from the boundaries of rhyme. America had not even produced a good blank-verse poet. Channing was caught in the quandary that appeared irresolvable before 1855: how to be free and spontaneous and still write poetry. He had come to maturity hearing the calls for a genuine American literature and for a freedom from European standards, but when he wrote, he could see few alternatives.

Emerson had the surest, most imaginative grasp of the problem, and in his essays he charted the course of a new American esthetic, but Whitman alone moved from theory to actual poems. Quite clearly prose, not poetry, became a fully developed art form for the Transcendentalists, one which could both preach and practice freedom from convention. If Emerson and Thoreau wrote poetry of marginal quality, their essays more than compensated.

But Channing could not compromise with his determination to be a poet, and so he rejected the alternative that prose offered Emerson and Thoreau. Channing was convinced that prose was not esthetically rewarding, for, to him, it did not stir the emotions nor create beauty as did poetry. For this reason, he could not perfect a "voice" for his prose; he never understood how to create a relationship between himself as an observer and his material other than in verse. All he could find was the clumsy device of "dramatic" dialogue that remains wooden and artificial. Only in his all-too-infrequent comments on Thoreau in *Thoreau: The Poet-Naturalist* does Channing create a supple, evocative prose.

Yet even with its limitations, Channing's prose reveals much about his milieu and about himself, for it is the record of a young man struggling with a literary vocation in the fertile years from 1840 to 1860. There is a cultural record in Channing's prose pieces in *The Dial* when his agonized young artists and writers struggle with their inner needs. The *Conversations in Rome* volume is typically American in its attempt to confront European art and society. *Thoreau: The Poet-Naturalist* is Channing's confession of faith in man's possibilities. Ellery Channing did not write prose often because he felt poetry was a more genuine form of art, but his three prose pieces come to terms with important literary and intellectual questions.

Being a poet was clearly a symbolic role for Channing that spoke to his deepest needs. While all the literary Transcendentalists honored the vocation of poet, only Channing invested all of his emotional energy in writing poems. Personally he needed the role because it turned his ideals of beauty and emotional stimulation into concrete activity. At its best, his work urges men on to more complete, more satisfying lives by focusing on nature and by rejecting materialism. Even without a faith in transcendent reality, this "casual" Transcendentalist turned his faith in men into poems.

In addition to this career as a poet, Channing became a friend whose conversation never ceased to amaze and delight and who used his talent to affect his friends. The writers of Channing's era lived in a highly oral culture: not only lyceum lectures, but formal and informal conversations were important forms of intellectual activity in a nation not yet able to support its best writers on a system of royalties. Though their books had small sales, Emerson, Alcott, and Margaret Fuller were able to make their way with their voices—on the lecture circuit. When, as in a conversation, the premium lay on spontaneity and wit, Channing was equal to Thoreau and Emerson in creating an imaginative language. When the relationship was most personal and private, his genius for imaginative intercourse was highest. For this reason, his friendships impress us as his most lasting contribution to our intellectual history. Paradox upon paradox emerges from his personal life, but none is perhaps so marked as the contradiction of the man who revered the life of a poet finally making his longest-lived contribution and effect as a friend. He was indifferent to metaphysical principles, so his poetry sometimes lagged; but he was so witty and imaginative in his daily contacts with his friends that he evoked talent in others.

Channing kept both Emerson and Thoreau from feeling wholly isolated. Each found him to be a sympathetic spirit; each found him stimulating. Thoreau took from him a special kind of love that embraced both a challenge to his principles of self-reliance and an affection for a man with such kindred principles. Emerson responded to Channing's eye for beauty and to his ability to respond with fullness and originality as they walked together. This career as a friend shows as little else can how interwoven among the Concord group were the need to withdraw and preserve one's distance from other men and the need to share their lives with each other. Friendship was more than ideal; through Channing it became a daily, immediate reality. Life was not so rich for Emerson and Thoreau that they could live without Ellery Channing; for few other men had as they admitted, the unique combination of temperament, talent, and wit their gray-eyed, enigmatic friend had.

Channing's habits of living and his tenacious ability to keep writing poetry made him a living symbol not only for Emerson and Thoreau but also for Margaret Fuller and Alcott. One characteristic of the Concord group of writers was their insistence that America was at last coming, as it should, to a fully unique literature. Channing, they thought, was one of the products of this new blooming of American talent. The fact that he was a man living according to his own principles, that he was a serious poet to whom writing was more than a mere trade made him stand out: he was an American original.

Yet, in spite of this close bond with Emerson, Thoreau, Margaret Fuller, and Alcott, Channing was the loneliest man in Concord. He felt more alienated than any of his contemporaries; the intrusion of technology and commerce into America's pastoral dream shattered Channing and made him the intense, often erratic, seldom predictable man that he was. As Leo Marx shows, both Emerson and Thoreau had the ability to accommodate the locomotive and all it stood for; but Channing struggled with his feeling of displacement and was seldom satisfied that he had resolved the tension between the machine and the garden.[3] Significantly, only *The Wanderer*, a late poem, comes to a complex, full reconcilation of attitudes toward the threatened American ideal. Thoreau had the reputation for being a hermit because he secluded himself for twenty-six months at Walden Pond, but Channing's seclusion was more complete, longer lasting, and less satisfying. Thoreau found in the symbols of the pond, the hut, and the woods the meanings of his existence that he had sought in retiring to Walden's solitude. Channing wrote often of his need to find those meanings, but he never reached the height of insight and resolution that Thoreau did. Channing's biography of his friend had the unique ability to show how Thoreau had lived an uncommon life: to others, he was just a recluse or just a writer of nature's beauty; but to Channing he was a man who had joined literature and life without leaving a visible seam.

Many men who knew Channing thought him a most abject failure. The son of two prominent families, he was miserably poor, unknown, and capricious. His family life was wretched; he seemed unable to lead a normally happy, secure life with his wife and children. But these facts are too limited. He was intensely aware of other standards of value which gave him satisfaction: he was a poet and a friend; he responded to a richly clad natural world. There were, to be sure, tensions, paradoxes, and frustrations in his life; but they gave him more often than not the energy to write and the need to be a friend to other writers. He was at once a representative young writer of the 1840's who responded strongly to Emerson's influence, and he was a writer of achievement whose work helps us understand the life of American pastoralism in the nineteenth century.

Channing celebrated life and had a faith that was grounded in the possibilities he recognized in man. Rose Hawthorne remembered her delight as a child when Channing invited her to go for a walk. "A man's high-water mark is his calibre," she says; "and at high-water mark Mr. Channing's sea was to us buoyant, richtinted, sunlit; a great force, darkening and dazzling with beautiful emotions."[4] With the emotional and moral strength that has characterized America's pastoral literature, Channing had faith in his vision of what man might have, of what he might be. The old, original sense of an Edenic reality in which man is free to choose his potential joy or his destruction was lively in Channing, whose bark was forever ready to sail, whose New England was ever a land of promise. The pastoral dream was becoming a nightmare to many men in the nineteenth century as the garden was forced further and further back into our history, as the past became the truth and the future only an illusion. But William Ellery Channing did not surrender to the change of a season: he lived his faith in man's consciousness.

Notes and References

Chapter One

1. Thomas Wentworth Higginson, MS. diary, December 25, 1901. Houghton.
2. Frederick T. McGill, Jr., *Channing of Concord* (New Brunswick, 1967), pp. 1–8; Franklin B. Sanborn, "Biographical Introduction," William Ellery Channing, *Poems of Sixty-Five Years* (Philadelphia and Concord, 1902), p. xiv.
3. McGill, p. 7.
4. Van Wyck Brooks, *The Flowering of New England* (New York, 1936), p. 34. For conditions at Harvard in the 1830's, see Samuel Eliot Morison, *Three Centuries of Harvard* (Cambridge, Mass., 1936), p. 260.
5. McGill, pp. 9–15.
6. *Ibid.*, p. 21.
7. Franklin B. Sanborn, "A Concord Note-Book: Ellery Channing and His Table Talk," *Critic*, XLVII (1905), 126.
8. Kathryn Whitford and Philip Whitford, "Ellery Channing in Illinois," *Wisconsin Academy of Sciences, Arts and Letters Transactions*, XLV (1956), 143–44.
9. *Ibid.*, p. 144; Sanborn, "Biographical Introduction," p. xxi.
10. Ralph Waldo Emerson, *The Letters of Ralph Waldo Emerson*, ed., Ralph L. Rusk (New York, 1939), II, 253.
11. *Ibid.*, 227.
12. *Ibid.*, 252–53.
13. *Ibid.*, 253.
14. *Ibid.*, 276.
15. *Ibid.*, 331.
16. McGill, pp. 35–38.
17. *Ibid.*, pp. 47–58.
18. *Ibid.*, pp. 53–54.
19. Emerson, *Letters*, II, 446.
20. McGill, p. 62.
21. Channing letter to Margaret Fuller, Sept. 5, 1841. Houghton.

22. Margaret Fuller letter to Channing, [Oct. 3, 1841]. Houghton.
23. McGill, p. 61.
24. Mrs. Fuller letter to Margaret Fuller, May 15, 1842. Houghton.
25. *Ibid.*
26. Channing letter to Margaret Fuller, Feb. 26, 1842. Houghton.
27. *Ibid.*
28. *Ibid.*
29. Channing letter to Margaret Fuller, Mar. 20, 1842. Houghton.
30. Emerson, *Letters*, II, 313.
31. Channing letter to Margaret Fuller, Mar. 20, 1842. Houghton.
32. Margaret Fuller, "Works," III, 159 ff. Houghton. The volumes in the Fuller Family Papers called "Works" are bound volumes of copied extracts from Margaret Fuller's manuscript letters, journals, and workbooks.
33. Julian Hawthorne, *Nathaniel Hawthorne and His Wife* (Boston and New York, 1884), I, 253.
34. Emerson, *Letters*, III, 267–68.
35. *Ibid.*, 174.
36. Nathaniel Hawthorne, *The American Notebooks*, ed. Randall Stewart (New Haven, 1932), p. 168.
37. Channing letter to Margaret Fuller, May 21, 1843. Houghton.
38. Edgar Allan Poe, "Our Amateur Poets," *Graham's Magazine*, XXIII (Aug., 1843), 113–17.
39. *Concord Massachusetts: Births, Marriages, and Deaths* (Concord, 1895), p. 398. For details of the family anguish, see Channing letter to Margaret Fuller, June 27, 1844. Houghton.
40. Emerson, *Letters*, III, 268; Greeley was suffering horribly from an outbreak of boils brought on by his exhaustion: "I was covered by them . . . often fifty or sixty at once, so that I could contrive no position in which to rest. . . ." Horace Greeley, *Recollections of a Busy Life* (New York, 1868), p. 167.
41. Margaret Fuller letter to Samuel G. Ward, Dec. 29, 1844. Houghton.
42. Channing letter to Emerson, Feb. 9, 1845. Huntington.
43. "The one who came from farthest to my lodge, through deepest snows and most dismal tempests, was a poet. . . . We made that small house ring with boisterous mirth and resound with the murmur of much sober talk. . . ." H. D. Thoreau, *Walden* (Boston and New York, 1893), p. 295.
44. Emerson, *Letters*, III, 327.
45. Channing letter to Henry Bellows, Feb. 19, 1846. Massachusetts Historical Association. Like Channing, Henry Whitney Bellows (1814–82) had attended Round Hill School. After degrees from Harvard, Bellows became minister of the First Unitarian Church in New York

City. He gained a reputation as a radical reformer. Later, he moved to the Church of All Souls and founded the *Christian Inquirer*.

46. Emerson, *Letters*, III, 327.

47. *Ibid.*, 340; Samuel Eliot Morison, *By Land and by Sea* (New York, 1953), p. 299.

48. *Concord Massachusetts: Births, Marriages, and Deaths*, p. 400.

49. Emerson, *Letters*, III, 351.

50. Channing letter to James Munroe Co., May 6, 1850. Morgan.

51. Emerson, *Letters*, III, 395.

52. Bronson Alcott, *The Journals of Bronson Alcott*, ed. Odell Shepard (Boston, 1938), p. 202.

53. *Concord Massachusetts: Births, Marriages, and Deaths*, p. 402.

54. Channing letter to Ellen Channing, [July, 1850]. Houghton.

55. Franklin B. Sanborn, "Biographical Introduction," p. xxix. Richard Herrnstadt, ed., *The Letters of A. Bronson Alcott* (Ames, Iowa, 1969), p. 163; Channing letter to Sarah Helen Whitman, Mar. 3, 1852. Brown.

56. Franklin B. Sanborn, *Recollections of Seventy Years* (Boston, 1909), II, 322–23.

57. Henry D. Thoreau, *The Journal of Henry D. Thoreau*, ed. Bradford Torrey and Francis H. Allen (Boston, 1906), III, 249.

58. Channing letter to Samuel G. Ward, May 20, [1853]. Houghton; Concord Vital Record Cards. Concord Free Public Library.

59. Rollo G. Silver, "Ellery Channing's Collaboration with Emerson," *American Literature*, VII (1935), 85.

60. Walter Harding, "Two F. B. Sanborn Letters," *American Literature*, XXV (1953), 232.

61. McGill, pp. 124–47. McGill explores the broken marriage in more detail.

62. Ellen Channing letter to Barbara Channing, June 4, [1853]. Houghton.

63. Mrs. Fuller letter to Ellen Channing, Nov. 19, 1853. Houghton.

64. Quoted by McGill, pp. 141; 147.

65. Channing notebook, Nov. 27, 1853. Houghton.

66. Thoreau, *Journal*, III, 98–99.

67. McGill, p. 142.

68. Franklin B. Sanborn, "William Ellery Channing and Daniel Ricketson," New Bedford *Mercury*, Aug. 7, 1907, p. 7.

69. Edward Channing, "Recollections of a Hitherto Truthful Man," ed. Alice Channing, Elizabeth Channing Fuller, and Willard Perrin Fuller, Jr. Unpublished manuscript autobiography and family records. P. 7.

70. Barbara Channing letter to M[ary Channing Higginson], [Sept. 22, 1856]. Houghton.

Chapter Two

1. Poe, "Our Amateur Poets," 117.
2. [Francis Bowen], "Nine New Poets," *North American Review,* LXIV (April, 1847), 414–15.
3. Thoreau, *Journal,* VII, 22.
4. Thomas Wentworth Higginson, *Letters and Journals of Thomas Wentworth Higginson,* ed. Mary Thatcher Higginson (Boston and New York, 1921), p. 42.
5. William Ellery Channing, "The Youth of the Poet and the Painter," *Dial,* IV (1844), 185.
6. Channing letter to Marston Watson, March 1, 1860. Concord Free Public Library.
7. *Ibid.*
8. T[homas] W[entworth] H[igginson], "Walks with Ellery Channing," *Atlantic Monthly,* XC, (1902), 32.
9. Ralph Waldo Emerson, *Journals of Ralph Waldo Emerson,* ed. Edward Waldo Emerson and Waldo Emerson Forbes (Boston and New York, 1909–14), IX, 62.
10. Julian Hawthorne, *Nathaniel Hawthorne and His Wife,* I, 432.
11. Emerson, *Journals,* VII, 303.
12. Thoreau, *Journal,* VI, 75.
13. Rose Hawthorne Lathrop, *Memories of Hawthorne* (Boston and New York, 1897), p. 419.
14. George F. Hoar, *Autobiography of Seventy Years* (New York, 1906), pp. 74–75.
15. Emerson, *Journals,* VI, 359.
16. Leo Marx, *The Machine in the Garden* (New York, 1964), p. 24.
17. David P. Edgell, "A Note on a Transcendental Friendship," *New England Quarterly,* XXIV (1951), 530.
18. Channing letter to Samuel G. Ward, Mar. 15, 1842. Houghton.
19. Channing letter to Marston Watson, n.d. Concord Free Public Library.
20. F. O. Matthiessen, *The James Family* (New York, 1947), p. 480.
21. Sanborn, *Recollections of Seventy Years,* II, 575.
22. Samuel Eliot Morison, *By Land and by Sea* (New York, 1953), pp. 299 ff. Morison discusses the Channing family life after Ellen's death. Edward Channing became a professor of American history at Harvard where he distinguished himself as a teacher and as the author of an ambitious history of the United States.
23. Channing undated letters to his sons. Houghton.
24. Edgell, p. 529.

25. Anna and Walton Ricketson, ed., *Daniel Ricketson and His Friends* (Boston and New York, 1902), p. 5.

26. *Ibid.*, p. 302.

27. Henry D. Thoreau, *The Correspondence of Henry David Thoreau*, ed., Walter Harding and Carl Bode (New York, 1958), p. 413; Sanborn, "William Ellery Channing and Daniel Ricketson," p. 8.

28. Alcott, *Journals*, p. 314.

29. *Ibid.*, pp. 314–15.

30. Channing letter to Margaret Fuller, Sept. 17, 1841. Houghton.

31. Higginson, "Walks," p. 33.

32. Walter Harding, *The Days of Henry Thoreau* (New York, 1965), p. 171 and *passim*. The 1849 trip to Cape Cod formed the basis for Thoreau's posthumous *Cape Cod*.

33. Thoreau, *Journal*, III, 98–99.

34. Sanborn, *Recollections*, II, 353.

35. *Ibid.*, 293.

36. Emerson, *Journals*, VIII, 75.

37. Morris U. Schappes, "The Letters of Emma Lazarus: 1868–1885," *Bulletin of the New York Public Library*, LIII (1949), 329.

38. Sanborn, *Recollections*, II, 386–87.

39. *Ibid.*, 387–88.

40. Alcott, *Journals*, p. 437.

41. Sanborn, *Recollections*, II, 396.

42. Francis H. Allen, *A Bibliography of Henry David Thoreau* (Boston and New York, 1908), pp. 17–18, 20, 77.

43. Franklin B. Sanborn, "Dates and Circumstances in Regard to the Coming of W. E. Channing to Live with F. B. Sanborn," MS. essay. Concord Free Public Library.

44. The Boston *Globe*, Dec. 16, Dec. 24, 1901; Franklin B. Sanborn letter to William T. Harris, Dec. 23, 1901, Concord Free Public Library; Middlesex *Patriot*, Dec. 27, 1901; Boston Evening *Transcript*, Nov. 12, 1921.

Chapter Three

1. Channing, "The Youth of the Poet and the Painter," *Dial*, IV (1844), 277.

2. *Ibid.*

3. *Ibid.*, 283.

4. *Ibid.*, 273.

5. *Ibid.*, 284.

6. *Ibid.*, 276.

7. *Ibid.*, 446.

8. *Ibid.*, 450.
9. *Ibid.*, 279.
10. *Ibid.*, 182–84.
11. *Ibid.*, 178.
12. *Ibid.*, 185.
13. *Ibid.*, 180.
14. William Ellery Channing, *Conversations in Rome: Between an Artist, a Catholic, and a Critic* (Boston, 1847), pp. 12–13.
15. *Ibid.*, p. 2.
16. *Ibid.*, p. 22.
17. *Ibid.*, p. 18.
18. *Ibid.*, p. 39.
19. *Ibid.*, p. 93.
20. *Ibid.*, p. 17.
21. *Ibid.*, pp. 30–31.
22. *Ibid.*, p. 7.
23. *Ibid.*, p. 16.
24. *Ibid.*, p. 28.
25. *Ibid.*, p. 124.
26. *Ibid.*, p. 32.
27. Nathaniel Hawthorne, *The Marble Faun* (Columbus, Ohio, 1968), p. 124.
28. Channing, *Conversations*, p. 90.
29. Ralph Waldo Emerson, William Henry Channing and James Freeman Clarke, eds., *Memoirs of Margaret Fuller Ossoli* (Boston, 1859; 1884), II, 97.
30. Ralph Waldo Emerson, *The Journals and Miscellaneous Notebooks of Ralph Waldo Emerson*, ed. Alfred R. Ferguson, Merton M. Sealts, Jr., and Ralph H. Orth (Cambridge, Mass., 1964–66), V, 202.
31. William Ellery Channing, *Thoreau: The Poet-Naturalist* (Boston, 1873), p. 18.
32. *Ibid.*, pp. 32–33.
33. *Ibid.*, p. 51.
34. *Ibid.*, p. 106.
35. *Ibid.*, p. 5.
36. *Ibid.*, p. 7.
37. Joel Porte, *Emerson and Thoreau: Transcendentalists in Conflict* (Middletown, Conn., 1965), p. 125.
38. *Ibid.*, p. 128.
39. Channing, *Thoreau: The Poet-Naturalist*, p. 111.
40. *Ibid.*, p. 33.
41. *Ibid.*, p. 109.
42. Channing, *Thoreau: The Poet-Naturalist*, p. 187.
43. *Ibid.*, p. 31.

44. *Ibid.*, p. 217.
45. *Ibid.*, p. 105.
46. *Ibid.*
47. *Ibid.*, p. 32.
48. *Ibid.*, p. 88.

Chapter Four

1. William Ellery Channing, *The Collected Poems of William El-lery Channing the Younger,* ed. Walter Harding (Gainesville, Fla., 1967), p. 151. This facsimile edition gathers together all but the *Journal of Speculative Philosophy* poems.
2. *Ibid.*, p. 298.
3. *Ibid.*, p. 169.
4. Emerson, *Journals,* VII, 540.
5. *Ibid.*, IX, 106.
6. Channing, *Collected Poems,* p. 163.
7. *Ibid.*, p. 133.
8. "New Poetry," *Dial,* I (1840), 222.
9. Marx, *The Machine in the Garden,* pp. 227–65.
10. Channing, *Collected Poems,* p. 58.
11. *Ibid.*, p. 889.
12. *Ibid.*, p. 246.
13. *Ibid.*, p. 160.
14. Lois Whitney, *Primitivism and the Idea of Progress* (Baltimore, 1934), p. xiv. Lovejoy's essay is printed as the introduction to Miss Whitney's book.
15. Franklin B. Sanborn, "Ellery Channing on the Mystery of Shake-peare," MS. essay. Concord Free Public Library.
16. Marx, p. 5.
17. *Ibid.*, p. 23.
18. Channing, *Collected Poems,* p. 279.
19. *Ibid.*, p. 103.
20. *Ibid.*, pp. 26–27.
21. *Ibid.*, p. 235.
22. *Ibid.*, pp. 398–99.
23. Marx, p. 25.
24. Channing, *Collected Poems,* p. 80.
25. *Ibid.*, pp. 81–82.
26. *Ibid.*, pp. 313–14.
27. *Ibid.*, p. 73.
28. *Ibid.*, p. 258.
29. *Ibid.*, p. 225.

30. William Ellery Channing, "The Sunset," *Journal of Speculative Philosophy*, XIII (1879), 349.
31. Channing, *Collected Poems*, pp. 315–16.
32. William Ellery Channing, *Conversations*, pp. x–xi.
33. Channing, *Collected Poems*, p. 998.
34. *Ibid.*, p. 71.
35. *Ibid.*, p. 855.
36. *Ibid.*, pp. 220–22.
37. *Ibid.*, p. 93.
38. *Ibid.*, pp. 96, 100.
39. *Ibid.*, p. 159.
40. William Ellery Channing, "On a Long Name," MS. poem. Houghton.
41. Channing, *Collected Poems*, p. 110.

Chapter Five

1. Channing, *Collected Poems of William Ellery Channing the Younger*, p. 436.
2. *Ibid.*, p. 437.
3. *Ibid.*, p. 429.
4. *Ibid.*, p. 428.
5. *Ibid.*, p. 421.
6. *Ibid.*, pp. 448–49.
7. *Ibid.*, p. 441.
8. Marx, *The Machine in the Garden*, p. 5.
9. Channing, *Collected Poems*, p. 462.
10. *Ibid.*, p. 461.
11. *Ibid.*, p. 462.
12. *Ibid.*, p. 489.
13. *Ibid.*, p. 484.
14. *Ibid.*, p. 515.
15. *Ibid.*, p. 547.
16. *Ibid.*, pp. 592–93.
17. *Ibid.*, p. 552.
18. *Ibid.*, p. 601.
19. *Ibid.*, p. 604.
20. *Ibid.*, p. 520.
21. *Ibid.*, p. 501.
22. *Ibid.*, pp. 534–35.
23. Channing letter to Sarah Helen Whitman, Nov. 3, 1852. Brown University.
24. Thoreau, *Journal*, XIII, 7.

25. Channing, *Collected Poems*, p. 825.
26. *Ibid.*, p. 764.

Chapter Six

1. Hawthorne, *The American Notebooks*, p. 168.
2. *Ibid.*
3. Julian Hawthorne, *Nathaniel Hawthorne and His Wife*, II, 264–65.
4. Sanborn, *Recollections of Seventy Years*, II, 531.
5. *Ibid.*, p. 532.
6. *Ibid.*, p. 526.
7. Nathaniel Hawthorne, *Mosses from an Old Manse* (Boston and New York, 1882), p. 35.
8. *Ibid.*
9. *Ibid.*
10. *Ibid.*
11. *Ibid.*, p. 36.
12. Hawthorne, *American Notebooks*, p. 312.
13. Franklin B. Sanborn, *Bronson Alcott at Alcott House England and Fruitlands, New England (1842–44)* (Cedar Rapids, Iowa, 1908), p. 36.
14. Herrnstadt, ed., *Letters of A. Bronson Alcott*, p. 163.
15. Alcott, *Journals*, p. 420.
16. *Ibid.*, p. 437.
17. *Ibid.*, p. 420.
18. *Ibid.*, pp. 268–69.
19. *Ibid.*, p. 104.
20. *Ibid.*, pp. 222–23.
21. A. Bronson Alcott, *Concord Days* (Philadelphia, 1872; 1962), p. 74.
22. Alcott, *Journals*, p. 269.
23. Thomas Wentworth Higginson, *Cheerful Yesterdays* (Boston and New York, 1898), p. 174.
24. Alcott, *Journals*, p. 220.
25. *Ibid.*, p. 269.
26. *Ibid.*
27. *Ibid.*, p. 227.
28. *Ibid.*, p. 422.
29. *Ibid.*, p. 253.
30. Alcott, *Concord Days*, p. 10.
31. Alcott, *Journals*, p. 188.
32. *Ibid.*, p. 220.

33. Quoted in John C. Broderick, "Bronson Alcott's 'Concord Book,'" *New England Quarterly*, XXIX (1956), 370.

34. Herrnstadt, p. 240.

35. Alcott, *Journals*, p. 364.

36. Channing letter to Margaret Fuller, 1842. Houghton.

37. Margaret Fuller, "Works," III, 175. Fuller Family Papers. Houghton.

38. Channing letter to Ellen Channing, [July], 1850. Houghton.

39. Emerson, *Journals*, VIII, 215.

40. Channing letter to Marcus Spring, June 5, 1851. University of Virginia.

41. Fuller, "Works," I, 431.

42. Emerson, Channing, and Clarke, *Memoirs*, I, 211; Sanborn, *Recollections*, II, 355.

43. Emerson, Channing, Clarke, *Memoirs*, I, 210.

44. *Ibid.*, 38.

45. *Ibid.*, 342.

46. *Ibid.*, 343–44.

47. *Ibid.*, 96.

48. *Ibid.*, 107.

49. *Ibid.*

50. *Ibid.*, 210.

51. Fuller, "Works," I, 597.

52. *Ibid.*

53. *Ibid.*, 403.

54. Emerson, Channing, Clarke, *Memoirs*, II, 28–29.

55. Channing letter to Ellen Channing, [July], 1850. Houghton.

56. Thoreau, *Journal*, I, 166.

57. *Ibid.*, IX, 479.

58. Henry D. Thoreau, *A Week on the Concord and Merrimack Rivers*, ed. Walter Harding (New York, 1963), p. 224.

59. Thoreau, *Journal*, I, 348.

60. Thoreau, *Week*, p. 227.

61. *Ibid.*, p. 226.

62. Thoreau, *Journal*, I, 340.

63. *Ibid.*, IV, 163.

64. Thoreau, *Week*, pp. 221; 223.

65. Thoreau, *Journal*, XI, 282.

66. Perry Miller, *Consciousness in Concord* (Boston, 1957), p. 91.

67. *Ibid.*, p. 89.

68. McGill, pp. 119–20.

69. See, for instance, Channing, *Thoreau: The Poet-Naturalist*, p. 105.

70. Thoreau, *Journal*, VIII, 231–32.

71. *Ibid.*, XI, 296–97.
72. Henry D. Thoreau, *The Writings of Henry David Thoreau* (Boston and New York, 1893), p. 252.
73. Thoreau, *Journal*, XI, 120.
74. *Ibid.*, V, 504.
75. *Ibid.*, XI, 393.
76. *Ibid.*, VII, 125.
77. *Ibid.*, III, 108.
78. *Ibid.*, V, 189–90.
79. Thoreau, *Correspondence*, p. 208.
80. Thoreau, *Journal*, I, 439.
81. *Ibid.*, IX, 216.
82. *Ibid.*, I, 340.
83. Ralph Waldo Emerson, *The Complete Works of Ralph Waldo Emerson*, ed. Edward Waldo Emerson (Boston and New York, 1903–4), II, 189.
84. *Ibid.*, 198.
85. Emerson, *Complete Works*, II, 208.
86. Emerson, *Journals*, X, 188–89.
87. Emerson, *Works*, II, 199.
88. Emerson, *Journals and Miscellaneous Notebooks*, IV, 271.
89. *Ibid.*
90. *Ibid.*, VI, 119.
91. Emerson, *Journals*, V, 173–74.
92. Emerson, *Journals and Miscellaneous Notebooks*, V, 363.
93. *Ibid.*, 54–55.
94. Higginson, "Walks," 30–31.
95. *Ibid.*, 33.
96. Emerson, *Journals and Miscellaneous Notebooks*, VI, 119.
97. Emerson, *Journals*, VIII, 252.
98. *Ibid.*, VII, 540.
99. *Ibid.*, 330.
100. *Ibid.*, 230–31.
101. *Ibid.*, IX, 448–49.
102. Emerson, *Letters*, III, 395.
103. *Ibid.*, IV, 199.
104. Emerson, *Journals*, VIII, 130.
105. *Ibid.*, VI, 234–35.
106. *Ibid.*, VII, 540.
107. Emerson, *Journals and Miscellaneous Notebooks*, V, 363.
108. Emerson, *Journals*, VI, 348.
109. *Ibid.*, VIII, 293.
110. Emerson, *Letters*, III, 102–3.
111. Thoreau, *Journal*, I, 352.

112. Emerson, *Journals*, IX, 183–84.
113. Emerson, *Letters*, III, 181.

Chapter Seven

1. Thoreau, *Journal*, III, 249.
2. Emerson, *Journals*, VII, 230.
3. Marx, *The Machine in the Garden*, pp. 229–65.
4. Rose Hawthorne Lathrop, *Memories of Hawthorne*, p. 419.

Selected Bibliography

Only one biography of Channing has been written: *Channing of Concord* by Frederick T. McGill (New Brunswick, New Jersey: Rutgers University Press, 1967). McGill's book appeared after I had completed my first study of Channing's life, but I have here been able to make use of his accurate work to correct myself on some minor points and to expand some details of Channing's family life; where possible, I have relied on manuscript sources for my interpretation of Channing's life. When these were incomplete, I turned to the writings of Emerson, Thoreau, Alcott, and Margaret Fuller. The bibliography of secondary sources is a guide to these writings and to general studies of the period.

Since McGill's study is a biography, I intend this one to be a complementary critical work. For additional details of Channing's early life and his marriage, the reader should consult *Channing of Concord*.

PRIMARY SOURCES

1. Books (in order of publication)

Poems. Boston: Little and Brown, 1843.
Poems: Second Series. Boston: James Munroe, 1847.
Conversations in Rome Between an Artist, a Catholic and a Critic. Boston: William Crosby, 1847.
The Woodman, and Other Poems. Boston: James Munroe, 1849.
Near Home, A Poem. Boston: James Munroe, 1858.
The Wanderer: A Colloquial Poem. Boston: James R. Osgood, 1871.
Thoreau: The Poet-Naturalist. Boston: Roberts Brothers, 1873. Revised and enlarged ed., F. B. Sanborn. Boston: Goodspeed, 1902.
Eliot. A Poem. Boston: Cupples, Uppham, 1885.
John Brown, and the Heroes of Harper's Ferry. A Poem. Boston: Cupples, Uppham, 1886.
Poems of Sixty-Five Years. Ed., F. B. Sanborn. Philadelphia and Concord: James H. Bentley, 1902.
The Collected Poems of William Ellery Channing the Younger. Ed., Walter Harding. Gainesville, Fla.: Scholars' Facsimiles, 1967.

2. Uncollected Poems

"Speculum Poesis," *Journal of Speculative Philosophy*, IX (1875), 186–90.

"Wigelia: An Ode to M. W. C.," *Journal of Speculative Philosophy*, XI (1877), 390–92.

"In Memoriam," *Journal of Speculative Philosophy*, XII (1878), 214–16.

"Cottage Hymns," *Journal of Speculative Philosophy*, XIII (1879), 346–51.

"Edith," *Journal of Speculative Philosophy*, XIX (1885), 102.

"A Dream—To Edith," *Journal of Speculative Philosophy*, XIX (1885), 102–3.

"In Memoriam, J.F.B.," *Journal of Speculative Philosophy*, XIX (1885), 219–20.

"A Tribute to the Heroes Grant and Garfield," *Journal of Speculative Philosophy*, XIX (1885), 429–32.

3. Manuscripts

Houghton Library, Harvard University:
   Ellery Channing papers (bMS Am 800.6): notebooks, miscellaneous manuscript poems, letters, and papers.
   Channing family papers (bMS Am 1610): manuscript poems, letters of Ellery, Ellen, Dr. Walter Channing, and others.
   Fuller family papers (fMS 1086): letters of Ellery and Ellen Channing, Margaret Fuller, and others.
   Tappan family papers (bMS Am 1221): manuscript poems, letters of Ellery Channing.
   Anna and Samuel G. Ward papers (bMS Am 1465): manuscript poems, letters.
   Ralph Waldo Emerson Memorial Association papers (bMS Am 1280): letters from Channing to Emerson.
Concord Free Public Library:
   Ninety-three letters from Ellery Channing to Mr. and Mrs. Marston Watson.
   Two Channing manuscript lectures on "Society."
   Two Channing manuscript books of poems.
   Two Channing manuscript prose satires: "Major Leviticus" and "Leviticus."
Massachusetts Historical Society:
   Extensive uncatalogued holdings of Channing family letters, journals, and memoranda. The material is interspersed among three large family collections (Channing, Minot, and Perkins).

Pierpont Morgan Library:
    Three Ellery Channing letters.
    Part of the 1853 "Country Walking" manuscript.
    Two Channing manuscript poems, "To Alcott," and "Morrice Lake."
Brown University Library:
    Five Channing letters to Sarah Helen Whitman.
    Copy of a letter from Miss Whitman to Channing.
    One Channing manuscript poem, "The Tippet."
University of Virginia Library. The Clifton Waller Barrett Library of American Literature:
    Letters from Ellery Channing to Marcus Spring and Miss Chandler.
    One untitled Channing manuscript poem.
Boston Public Library:
    Ellery Channing letters to James Munroe Co. and Mrs. S. Coleman.
Henry Huntington Library:
    Letters from Ellery Channing to Emerson and W. T. Fields.
New York Public Library:
    Two Ellery Channing letters to unidentified persons.
University of Texas Library:
    One Channing manuscript poem, "O Golden Green."
Chicago Historical Society:
    One Channing manuscript poem, "The Burial Of John Brown."

SECONDARY SOURCES

ALCOTT, A. BRONSON. *Concord Days.* Boston: Roberts Brothers, 1872.
———. *The Journals of Bronson Alcott.* Ed. Odell Shepard. Boston: Little, Brown, 1938.
———. *The Letters of A. Bronson Alcott.* Ed. Richard L. Herrnstadt. Ames, Iowa: Iowa State University Press, 1969.
BROOKS, VAN WYCK. *The Flowering of New England.* New York: Dutton, 1936. History of the pre-Civil War era in New England. Discusses Channing briefly and the major writers at length. Very limited critical discussion.
BROWN, ARTHUR W. *Margaret Fuller.* New York: Twayne, 1964. Short but careful assessment of Channing's sister-in-law.
CARGILL, OSCAR. "Nemesis and Nathaniel Hawthorne," *Publications of the Modern Language Association,* LII (1937), 848–62. Fanciful speculation about Channing's relationship to Hawthorne and Margaret Fuller. Answered convincingly by Randel (see below).

DEDMOND, E. B. "William Ellery Channing on Thoreau: An Unpublished Satire," *Modern Language Notes,* LXVII (1952), 50–52. Portion of the "Major Leviticus" manuscript.

EDGELL, DAVID P. "A Note on a Transcendental Friendship," *New England Quarterly,* XXIV (1951), 528–32. Contains letters from Channing to Elizabeth Hoar concerning Emerson.

ELLIS, CHARLES MAYO. *An Essay on Transcendentalism.* Ed. Walter Harding. Gainesville, Fla.: Scholars' Facsimiles, 1954. Early, perceptive history of Transcendentalism.

EMERSON, RALPH WALDO. *The Complete Works of Ralph Waldo Emerson.* Ed. Edward Waldo Emerson. Boston and New York: Houghton Mifflin, 1903–4.

————. *The Journals and Miscellaneous Notebooks of Ralph Waldo Emerson.* Eds. Alfred R. Ferguson, Merton M. Sealts, Jr., and Ralph H. Orth. Cambridge, Mass.: Harvard University Press, 1964–69.

————. *Journals of Ralph Waldo Emerson.* Ed. Edward Waldo Emerson and Waldo Emerson Forbes. Boston and New York: Houghton Mifflin, 1909.

————. *Letters from Ralph Waldo Emerson to a Friend: 1838–1853.* Ed. C. E. Norton. New York: Houghton Mifflin, 1899.

————. *The Letters of Ralph Waldo Emerson.* Ed. Ralph L. Rusk. New York: Columbia University Press, 1939.

FROTHINGHAM, OCTAVIUS B. *Transcendentalism in New England.* New York: Putnam, 1876. Most complete study of American Transcendentalism.

GOODMAN, PAUL. "Ethics and Enterprise: The Values of a Boston Elite, 1800–1860," *American Quarterly,* XVIII (1966), 437–51. Gives cogent view of the materialism against which Channing reacted.

HARDING, WALTER. *The Days of Henry Thoreau.* New York: Knopf, 1965. Very handy collection of facts about Channing and Thoreau.

————. "Two F. B. Sanborn Letters," *American Literature,* XXV (1953), 230–34. On Channing's preparation of the 1853 "Country Walking" manuscript.

HAWTHORNE, JULIAN. *Nathaniel Hawthorne and His Wife.* Boston and New York: Houghton Mifflin, 1884. Valuable recollections of Sophia Hawthorne's friendship with Channing.

HAWTHORNE, NATHANIEL. *The American Notebooks.* Ed. Randall Stewart. New Haven, Conn.: Yale University Press, 1932. Records many impressions of Channing in his journal.

HENNESSEY, HELEN. " 'The Dial': Its Poetry and Poetic Criticism," *New England Quarterly,* XXXI (1958), 66–87. Discussion of the critical concepts being discussed as Channing began his career.

HIGGINSON, THOMAS WENTWORTH. "Walks With Ellery Channing," *Atlantic Monthly*, XC (1902), 27–34. Excerpts from Emerson's journal about Channing and his conversational wit; many anecdotes previously unpublished.

LATHROP, ROSE HAWTHORNE. *Memories of Hawthorne*. Boston and New York: Houghton Mifflin, 1897. Hawthorne's daughter recalls Channing; very helpful contemporary view.

MARX, LEO. *The Machine in the Garden*. New York: Oxford University Press, 1964. Complete discussion of the pastoral theme in American literature.

MATTHIESSEN, F. O. *American Renaissance*. New York: Oxford University Press, 1941. Standard, most influential critical discussion of the period.

MILLER, PERRY. *The Transcendentalists*. Cambridge, Mass.: Harvard University Press, 1950. Extensive source book of writings by Channing's Transcendental friends and contemporaries. Excellent essay by Miller on the movement.

MORISON, SAMUEL E. *By Land and by Sea*. New York: Knopf, 1953. Contains a biographical essay on Edward Channing, Ellery's youngest child, who was Morison's teacher at Harvard. Witty as well as informative.

OSSOLI, MARGARET FULLER. *Memoirs of Margaret Fuller Ossoli*. Ed. R. W. Emerson, W. H. Channing, and J. F. Clarke. Boston: Roberts Brothers, 1884.

———. *The Writings of Margaret Fuller*. Ed. Mason Wade. New York: Viking, 1941.

POE, EDGAR ALLAN. "Our Amateur Poets," *Graham's Magazine*, XXIII (1843), 113–17. Scathing review of Channing's *Poems*.

PORTE, JOEL. *Emerson and Thoreau: Transcendentalists in Conflict*. Middletown, Conn.: Wesleyan University Press, 1966. Only full study of intellectual differences between the two main Transcendentalists.

RANDEL, W. P. "Hawthorne, Channing, and Margaret Fuller," *American Literature*, X (1939), 472–76. Rebuttal of Cargill (see above).

RICKETSON, ANNA and WALTON RICKETSON, eds. *Daniel Ricketson and His Friends*. Boston and New York: Houghton Mifflin, 1902. Contains letters to Thoreau about Channing. Excerpts from Ricketson's diary about Channing. Valuable contemporary account of the poet.

RICKETSON, DANIEL. *New Bedford of the Past*. Ed. Anna and Walton Ricketson. Boston and New York: Houghton Mifflin, 1903. More recollections of Channing by Ricketson, his friend and sympathetic admirer.

Rusk, Ralph L. *The Life of Ralph Waldo Emerson.* New York: Scribner's, 1949. Standard Emerson biography; many details given of the friendship with Channing.

Sanborn, Franklin B. *Bronson Alcott at Alcott House England and Fruitlands, New England (1842–44).* Cedar Rapids, Iowa: Torch Press, 1908. Contains letters of Channing describing Alcott and his ventures.

———. "Channing's Verse," *Nation,* LXXVI (1903), 10. One of Sanborn's many attempts to build Channing's reputation.

———. "A Concord Note-Book," *Critic,* XLVII (1905), 76–81, 121–28, 267–72, 444–51. Extensive, valuable recollection of Sanborn's friendship with Channing. Record of many of their conversations.

———. "Dates and Circumstances in Regard to the Coming of William Ellery Channing to Live with Franklin B. Sanborn." Typed essay of Sanborn's. Concord Free Public Library.

———. "Ellery Channing and John Brown," *Massachusetts Historical Society Proceedings,* XLIII (1910), 290–95.

———. "Ellery Channing in New Hampshire," *Granite Monthly,* XXXII (1902), 157–64.

———. "Ellery Channing on the Mystery of Shakespeare. With a Sketch of the Essayist." Typed essay. Concord Free Public Library.

———. "Emerson and Contemporary Poets," *Critic,* XLII (1903), 414. Discussion of Emerson and his contemporaries.

———. "The Maintenance of a Poet," *Atlantic Monthly,* LXXXVI (1900), 819–25. Details of Channing's later life.

———. "Notes on William Ellery Channing. August 28, 1901 to September 17, 1901." Typed essay describing Channing and his habits. Concord Free Public Library.

———. *Recollections of Seventy Years.* Boston: R. G. Badger, 1909. Most extensive discussion of Channing before McGill's biography. Sanborn is exasperatingly careless and cavalier with his facts. Although, of all of Channing's friends, his memoirs are most extensive and ambitious, he frequently leads the reader astray factually and allows his intense loyalty to Channing to mar his critical assessment. Still, this autobiography (and his other writings) is indispensable for a biographical, critical, or intellectual history of the Concord literary group.

———. "Was Ellery Channing a Knave?" Defense of Channing whose reputation in Concord was bad. Typed essay. Concord Free Public Library.

———. "William Ellery Channing and Daniel Ricketson," New Bedford *Mercury,* August 7, 1907, pp. 7–8. Details of Channing's life in New Bedford.

SHEPARD, ODELL. *Pedlar's Progress: The Life of Bronson Alcott*. Boston: Little, Brown, 1937. Standard biography; details of the friendship with Channing.

SILVER, ROLLO G. "Ellery Channing's Collaboration With Emerson," *American Literature*, VII (1935), 84–86. Further details of the "Country Walking" project.

STRAUCH, CARL F. "Hatred's Swift Repulsions: Emerson, Margaret Fuller, and Others," *Studies in Romanticism*, VII (1968), 65–103. Discussion of several of Channing's friends. Very cogent essay on Transcendental friendship.

THOREAU, HENRY D. *The Correspondence of Henry D. Thoreau*. Ed. Walter Harding and Carl Bode. New York: New York University Press, 1958.

———. *The Journal of Henry D. Thoreau*. Ed. Bradford Torrey and Francis H. Allen. Boston and New York: Houghton Mifflin, 1906.

———. *A Week on the Concord and Merrimack Rivers*. Ed. Walter Harding. New York: Holt, Rinehart, Winston, 1963.

———. *The Writings of Henry David Thoreau*. Boston: Houghton Mifflin, 1894.

WAGGONER, HYATT H. *American Poets From the Puritans to the Present*. Boston: Houghton Mifflin, 1968. Good chapter on Emerson and his influence on American poetry.

WHITFORD, KATHRYN and PHILLIP WHITFORD. "Ellery Channing in Illinois," *Wisconsin Academy of Sciences, Arts and Letters Transactions*, XLV (1956), 143–47. Details about Channing's life on the prairie.

WILLIAMS, PAUL O. "Emerson Guided: Walks with Thoreau and Channing," *Emerson Society Quarterly*, No. 35 (1964), pp. 66–68.

———. "The Transcendental Movement in American Poetry." Doctoral dissertation, University of Pennsylvania, 1962. Sets Channing in relation to the Transcendentalists. Finds a close relationship between his writing and that of his contemporaries.

WILSON, JOHN B. "The Aesthetics of Transcendentalism," *Emerson Society Quarterly*, No. 57 (1969), pp. 27–34. Useful discussion of the theories current during Channing's early career.

Index

Channing, Ellery (*Continued*)
reliance, 94–100, 151; urban life,
42–44, 56, 66–67, 79–82, 84–86,
90, 93–94, 103–12, 131, 152
WRITINGS OF:
"The Arched Stream," 90
"The Barren Moors," 87–89
"The Benighted Traveller," 86–87
"The Bridges," 78
"The Burial of John Brown," 114
*Conversations in Rome between an
Artist, A Catholic and a Critic*,
32, 41, 60–67, 69, 74, 93, 111,
154
"Country Walking," 34–35, 50,
67–68, 124
"The Earth Spirit," 83–84
Eliot, 41, 103, 112–13
"Emerson," 94
"Hymn of the Earth," 77
*John Brown and the Heroes of
Harper's Ferry*, 41, 103, 113–15
"The Lonely Road," 95–98
"The Mountains," 84
Near Home, 41, 103–7, 109, 111,
112
"New England," 77–78, 81
"October," 83
"On a Long Name," 101
"On Receiving Some Drawings,"
95
"Our Birth Days," 89
Poems of Sixty-Five Years, 52
Poems: First Series, 30, 41, 76, 86,
98
Poems: Second Series, 33, 77, 95
"A Poet's Hope," 99
"Reverence," 80
"The River," 87
"Society," 151
"The Sibyl to her Lover," 98–99
"The Sunset," 90
"Theme for a World-Drama," 95
Thoreau: The Poet-Naturalist, 36,
49–51, 57, 60, 65, 67–73, 111,
112, 138, 154, 156
"To Readers," 83
"To the Reader," 93–94
"Una," 101

"Wachusett," 80, 89–90
"Walden," 91–92
"Walden Spring," 84–86, 87, 104
The Wanderer, 41, 52, 103, 107–
12, 156
The Woodman, 33
"The Youth of the Poet and the
Painter," 53–60, 64, 69, 74
Channing, Giovanni Eugene, 35
Channing, Margaret Fuller, 30
Channing, Walter, 18, 19, 24, 25,
37, 39–40, 45–46
Channing, Walter (Ellery's son), 34,
52
Channing, William Ellery, D. D., 18,
41
Channing, William Henry, 21, 54,
129
Chardon Street Convention, 75
Chicago, 21
Cincinnati *Gazette*, 24, 26
Clarke, James Freeman, 54, 129, 131
Clay, Henry, 31
Cogswell, Joseph G., 19
Comte, Auguste, 113
Concord Club, 125
Cushing, John, 32

Darwin, Charles, 113
The Dial, 21–24, 41, 53, 59, 75, 79,
83, 95, 120, 128, 154
Dwight, Josiah, 20, 21

Ellery, William, 18
Emerson, Ralph Waldo, 17, 18, 21–
24, 25, 26, 27, 28, 29, 30, 31–32,
33, 35–36, 38, 41, 42–45, 46, 47,
49, 50, 51, 52, 54, 57, 59, 66, 71,
75, 76, 78, 79, 83, 86, 91, 94, 98,
100–101, 111–12, 113, 115, 116,
120, 121, 122, 123, 124, 128, 129,
130, 132, 133, 136, 141, 142–51,
152–57; theory of conversation,
143–44, 148; theory of friendship,
142–44, 148–49; "Friendship,"
142–43; "Divinity School Address," 75; *Nature*, 22, 75, 82;
"New Poets," 79

Shakespeare, William, 121
Spencer, Herbert, 113
Spring, Marcus, 129
Sturgis, Caroline, 26, 32, 54, 148
Swedenborg, Emanuel, 101

Thoreau, Henry David, 17, 18, 21,
26, 29, 30, 31, 33, 34, 35, 36, 38,
39, 41–44, 46, 47–51, 52, 57, 59,
60, 67–73, 76, 78, 86, 90–92, 93,
94, 100–101, 102, 105–6, 111–
12, 113–15, 116, 120, 122, 123,
124–25, 126, 127, 133–42, 143,
147, 148, 149, 150–51, 152–57;
theory of friendship, 133–37, 150;
Cape Cod, 50, 163; "Days and
Nights in Concord," 51; *The
Maine Woods,* 50; *Walden,* 31,
46, 67, 68, 82, 160; *A Week
on the Concord and Merrimack
Rivers,* 68, 134, 135

Thoreau, Sophia, 50–51
Ticknor, George, 19
Town and Country Club, 123–24
Transcendentalism, 21, 38–39, 57,
69, 72–73, 75–76, 79, 83, 94, 99,
100–101, 103, 108, 112–13, 115,
116, 119, 121–22, 123, 133, 136,
137, 149–50, 152–57

Very, Jones, 39, 119–20, 148
Virgil, 82, 85

Ward, Samuel Gray, 22, 25, 30, 31–
32, 44, 45, 121, 129, 148
Wasson, David A., 121
Watson, Marston, 35, 42, 44
Western Messenger, 21
Whitman, Sarah Helen, 121
Whitman, Walt, 82, 98, 151, 153;
Leaves of Grass, 82, 153
Wordsworth, William, 20